*Unlock the Hidden Meaning
of Your Dreams
and Discover:*

* Why most divorce dreams manifest themselves as a badly run-down house, or a house that needs reconstruction or redecoration.

* How to use an anxiety dream—in which you wake up sweating, unnerved, and on edge—to gain insight into your deep and unspoken fears.

* Why exceptionally grounded, burdened, or serious people often experience flying dreams—which signify a desire to lighten up, escape, and be free!

* Hundreds of dream symbols, including: basement (unconscious), dancing (sexual activity), handbag (self identity), parked car (dead person), queen (mother), skating (avoidance).

PLUS—the worst nightmares for actors, lawyers, athletes, musici_____

D0834720

DREAM KEYS

Unlocking
the Power
of Your
Unconscious Mind

LAUREN LAWRENCE

A Dell Book

Published by
Dell Publishing
a division of
Random House, Inc.
1540 Broadway
New York, New York 10036

Dell books may be purchased for business or promotional use or for special sales. For information please write to: Special Markets Department, Random House, Inc., 1540 Broadway, New York, N.Y. 10036.

The trademark Dell® is registered in the U.S. Patent and Trademark Office.

ISBN: 0-440-23477-8

Designed by Susan Yuran

Printed in the United States of America

Published simultaneously in Canada

July 1999

10 9 8 7 6 5 4 3 2 1

OPM

To my son, Graham—
my noblest dream

to Ludovic Autet
in loving memory

and to dreamers
everywhere

ACKNOWLEDGMENTS

Profuse thanks to Sigmund Freud for having written his re-markable *Interpretation of Dreams,* and to my parents for having bought it and made it readily accessible on the book-shelf. Profound thanks to my psychiatrist and psychoanalyst, the late Dr. Gerald Freiman. A debt of gratitude to the dark-ness of the evening—the dream time—and to every dreamer who has told me a dream.

Special thanks to Michael Douglas for having given me my first celebrity dream—to Heather Cohane for inspiring me on my *Quest* for famous dreams to analyze—to Antonia de Portago, my first dreamer, to Mort Zuckerman, for my former *New York Daily News* column. Grateful thanks to all the publicists who assisted me in gaining access to the elu-sive dreams of their illustrious clients—especially to Stan Rosenfeld, Louise Spinner, Tia Ernst, and Johnny Planco. Special thanks to Winston Churchill for informing me of his grandfather's book, *The Dream*—to Larry Geller, who so generously related to me a never before published dream that Elvis Presley had shared with him—to Arthur Loeb of Madi-son Avenue Bookshop. Heartfelt thanks to Joey Reynolds, Victoria Jones, G. Gordon Liddy, and Barry Farber for hav-ing me on their radio shows.

My thanks to Yusha Auchincloss for entrusting me with the memory of Jacqueline Bouvier's dream, for sharing his own wonderful dreams, and for helping me get my "Dreams" column started in *Newport This Week*—to David Lauren, my former publisher at *Swing*—to my son, Graham, to my friends Liba Icahn, Laura Hunt, Martha Kramer, John Davis, Carmen, and especially Tommy, Alex, Joan, and Martin, for their helpful insights.

I am deeply grateful to my agent, Liz Berney, for her guidance, her faith and belief in me—to my dear friend Ludovic Autet for the dream that he was—whose friendship was an inspiration in the writing of this book—and to everyone at Dell. My utmost thanks to my visionary editor, Diane Bartoli.

Lauren Lawrence
New York, N.Y.
January 25, 1999

CONTENTS

PREFACE

)

Dreams are mysterious Muslim women half-submerged in the shadowed doorways of some Moroccan evening, the body of their significance veiled in the garment of a foreign fabric. Eyes peering from behind dark purdahs of secrecy—they do not reveal themselves completely but rather seduce time out of its place, out of its continuity. This disguise, this intrigue, is the charm of dreams.

I confess. I'm a dream junkie. But there are a lot of us around, bleary-eyed, pen in hand, feverishly scribbling in the dark privacy of our bedrooms. Addicted to fantasy you say? Hah! Handling the truth is more like it. There are those who would rather silence the drums and thunder of a distant war. But I, for one, am asking for favors by settling back in the cool trenches of memory to watch the fireworks enliven and intensify a distilled copy of the sky. My only discomfort is that the show is over too soon—with no curtain calls.

Dreams are provocateurs, contortionists, magicians skilled at sleight of hand. They speak volumes in an exotic tongue—chisel their hieroglyphics of metaphors and symbols. But within this silent yet audible communication between the unconscious and conscious mind is poignancy. For, dreams present what cannot be pictured directly, by often synthesizing several ideas into a solitary image—the way a cartouche often combines several hieroglyphic symbols. A dream displaces feelings from one idea to another—from one person to the next—like a bee pollinates.

Dreams are free-speech advocates, representatives of the Freedom of Information Act—uncensored and unrestricted by the demands of the ego and the intellect, unfettered by societal rules and regulations.

Dreams have been viewed as divine inspirations, but while the Bible makes many historical references to visions or prophecies wherein heavenly messages were received while people were sleeping, most dreams are nothing more than our own mundane creations, with contents derived from the trivial antecedents of the previous day. . . . Yet, with the directorial panache of a Hitchcock or a Fellini, the unconscious voraciously and attentively refocuses on what may have appeared inconsequential material and manages to prove even this almost revelatory.

It is not inappropriate to say that dreams are muses—having elicited great inventions, poetry, musical compositions, paintings, and films: from Coleridge's Xanadu to Elias Howe's sewing needle, from Mozart's and Schumann's concertos to the surrealist landscapes of Matta and Dali. And problem solvers—they resemble the fabled shoemaker's elves that got the task done while the cobbler was sleeping. The dreamer may appear to be on the sidelines watching from afar, but he or she is directing, producing, scriptwriting, editing, designing, and acting, sometimes playing *all* the parts. A dream is a tour-de-force performance.

Dreams are elusive phenomena that must be cupped in the hands of memory—their fragile painted wings pinned down in an effort of reflection—or they will fly where we cannot follow. Everyone dreams—but not everyone recalls their dreams upon awakening. Those that are remembered are easily forgotten, like the smell of perfume after it dissipates— which is why they must be written down immediately.

If we may say that dreams are newborn creations with a life of their own—I have on occasion given the slap that makes them breathe. In some cases I have been thrown a bone and asked to produce the whole skeleton. I have interpreted many dream narratives herein, but these analyses in no way preclude any other existing interpretation. In other words, there is no *one* definitive interpretation of a dream, as dreams are composed of many stories, narratives, and symbols unique to the dreamer.

When I was ten years old I remember taking down a dusty copy of Freud's *Interpretation of Dreams* from my parents' bookshelf—I remember it was a long night. I recall being fascinated as I thumbed my way through the many varied dream explications to figure out the meaning of my own childhood dreams. I was in awe of Freud's decoding abilities. This was spy stuff and I was Mata Hari wanting to know what demons I was releasing into the night.

Years later I found my own bearded, bespectacled, pipe-smoking, ancient artifact-collecting Freud in the brilliance of Dr. Gerald Freiman, psychiatrist and psychoanalyst extraordinaire, to whom I owe a profound nonrepayable debt of gratitude. He showed me how to decode the mystery of dreams and I haven't been able to stop since.

PART I

While
You
Were
Sleeping

1

Learning Your Unconscious

If we had to give a name to the present era, it would be termed the Computer or Digital Age or the Age of Information. Make no mistake, the computer is our lord and master nonpareil. Hark! *But there is life after computer!* In that the human brain is recognized as being our greatest computer bank, the human memory is our RAM or database system. The unconscious is the *mother lode* of our hard-drive space. Our technology for recording our dreams is paper and pen.

Recalling a dream is like opening a window in our operating system and attaching a file. With consciousness, as the addressee, all we have to do is click on *send*. We spend approximately one third of our lives sleeping—one out of every three hours in a state of unconsciousness. According to Jung, the unconscious (our hard-drive space) has processed and stored every bit of information that we have ever known or perceived in the course of our conscious lifetime. The unconscious is just plain smarter than the conscious mind because it does not forget, filter, or dilute information to make it more acceptable to our sensitive psyches. The unconscious does not pull any punches—it tells it like it is. The bruises remain unbandaged. The black and blues remain decidedly black and blue. But then the meddling ego or consciousness comes along like a worrisome grandmother with all sorts of protective mediations: heavy wads of gauze, veils, masks, and screens. These are the rationalizations, denials, modifications, and adaptations of the conscious mind that keep us from learning the real meanings of our dreams—our true feelings are distorted at the price of discretion. Like an adolescent at a bar we are not given the real stuff. It's Shirley Temples all the way. We are being placated by our conscious minds and we do not even know it. This necessitates that we consciously and actively learn to perform many functions, to decode and disrobe these disguises and wipe away the greasepaint. We must decipher these distortions, which is what psychoanalysis is all about—*for to access the unconscious is to gain power.*

Psychoanalysis is thriving because so many people want to find out why they think the things they think and do the things they do and to better understand their anxieties and depressions. We want to know why we are feeling unmotivated, frustrated, or uninspired; we want to keep wrong life choices from reoccurring; we want to eliminate conflict, to nourish our emotional lives, to enliven our sexual forays—all to gain a sense of control over our lives. But the unconscious can be the greatest therapist of all as it knows all the answers. There is no repression present, no resistance, the instincts are preserved intact—the trick is to know the office hours and to book early. We must learn the unconscious, and learning it on our own terms, in our own homes, away from the therapeutic situation can be incredibly empowering.

Let us begin by understanding how unconsciousness differs from consciousness. Simply put, unconsciousness is a manifestation of *objectivity,* whereas consciousness is a manifestation of *subjectivity.* The conscious self is the ''I'' which is necessarily subjective, and the unconscious self is the "not I" observing our wakefulness. Thus, the unconscious can be viewed as an objective presence. The unconscious is watchful—taking notes during every hour of our consciousness. It has to be up and operational to gather all the information we take in. Imagine it is our tennis coach seated behind the baseline. It knows when our toss is too low, or when we do not follow through on our forehand; it knows when we take our eye off the ball. While engaged in playing the sport of life we cannot assess what we are doing wrong. We are the player. The unconscious is our invaluable teacher ready to give us an objective view of ourselves, and it is available to us through our dreams. Being objective is the key to winning the game—the key to self-empowerment.

Learning the unconscious is a way to tap the unknown potential within us all. Tapping into the unconscious is to be aware of the influences and inspirations coming from this deeper realm inside of our brains that expresses itself in terms of fears, aspirations, creative ideas, inhibitions, regrets, and that determines our conscious wakeful emotional lives. Learning the unconscious enables us to thumb through our Table of Conscience and look up our self-justifications.

Consciousness means to perceive things, to be. In sleep the "I" fades, or, to be more specific, the identification with the "I" disappears, so that we lose track of our wakeful identities—our egos—along with the various personas or masks we put on, and the defenses we flourish. In this egoless state we are oblivious to our physical selves and our external sensual environmental surroundings.

We are already aware that consciousness is everywhere in the world—but as consciousness is everywhere so is unconsciousness. Yet, whereas consciousness is diffused by all the distracting mental or sensory stimuli, unconsciousness is lucid, which is why we must establish a connection with our most brilliant organ—our brain. We must learn how to access our internal computer while we are sleeping so as to get to all our organizational files.

In other words, unconsciousness is just another form of consciousness that when awake we are unaware of. Our internal unconscious maintains an unobtrusive existence until anxieties mount and assert themselves or make themselves known, preventing the continuance of sleep. Our dreams are *spillout*—the repressed material of the unconscious that has flowed into our external consciousness or awareness.

Our dreams reveal our inner core—our defense system. We must know our armies' positions in order to feed and nourish them, in order to regroup when necessary, to send the message to enter the mud-packed trenches when prudent. We must do battle courageously and be proud to wear wound stripes when we are hurt, but we must never pull back, retreat, or head for the hills. For understanding our dreams is a forward process, a progression bent on success. Only when we can command our inner brigade will we become masters of our own fate. And only then will we truly experience self-empowerment. But first we must obliterate *repression!*

The following is an example of a dream within a dream wherein a former patient of mine dreamt that he was having a nightmare. The dreamer saw himself lying in bed, tossing, turning, and silently screaming that he wanted to wake up—but hard as he tried he could not wake. The scream is insidious in that it goes unheard—a clever metaphor for repression. For the duration of the nightmare the dreamer felt immobilized and *powerless*—stuck in his horrible *unheard* and unnamed torment. After what felt like hours of screaming he finally awakened feeling emotionally depleted and exhausted. The wish of the dream was *to wake up*—the dream symbolized that the dreamer was aware of all that he was repressing. To prevent the dream from recurring the dreamer realized that he had to give *voice* to the repressed material of his dreams. He had to *learn his unconscious.*

REPRESSION: IF THE PANTS ARE CREASED—RE-PRESS 'EM

The wrinkled pair of pants that is deemed unsuitable for wearing is immediately sent off to the dry cleaners where the creases are meticulously flattened away, steamed out by a hot iron. If we substitute guilt, shame or anxiety for wrinkles, and the defense mechanism of censorship for the hot iron we have a working understanding of the machinery of repression. The creases and wrinkles are the results of our wakeful movements and activities—the wear and tear of our personal existence. The pair of pants will return from the cleaners looking brand new and unworn by our bodies; the stretched out shapes that our knees made in the legs are gone. But in the case of repression, the pants never return from the dry cleaners. This is the meaning of repression.

Repression is a phenomenon. It is a *response* process— the act of rejecting aversive thoughts from consciousness. It is thought inhibition. Repression, if asked, will tell us that it allays our psychic pain, as a defense mechanism. But the problem with repression is that it indiscriminately represses elements around the one it is focusing on as well. (In other words, it sends a freshly pressed shirt to the dry cleaners along with creased pants in the assumption that the pressed shirt will remind us of the un-wearable condition of the pants.) Well, there goes another shirt we'll never see again. Another problem with repression is that it requires a great expenditure of energy to keep itself activated—our energy. Not to mention that it robs us of a unique piece of ourselves.

THE GHOST IN THE MACHINE

The ghost in the machine is the return of the repressed material (of the unconscious), which has come back, like Hamlet's father, to haunt consciousness. With the emergence of the repressed, the territory of the unconscious is decreased and the boundaries of consciousness are broadened. By becoming aware of our internal dominating unconscious, our reality is better perceived. By figuring out what we have repressed through the interpretative application of dream analysis we are to a great extent increasing our personal awareness.

Dreams have the very real function of uncovering the unconscious contents—of *spilling the beans*—in order to expose them to the light of day (or consciousness), which, as previously stated, minimizes the expenditure of energy it takes to keep something buried (repressed). Freud has mentioned an "upward drive" of the unconscious. Imagine trying to keep a bar of soap at the bottom of our bath without the pressure of our hand on top of it keeping it submerged. The moment we take the pressure off—the soap rises to the top. Our unconscious works much the same way.

As repression is stored material—and there is lots of it— the material is cramped and contorted and therefore distorted (as it manifests itself in our dreams), but it is a part of our personality, nonetheless, that we are entitled to behold. We need to deal with our anxious thoughts; we need to recognize our guilt and discuss our shame and our fear. Imagine for one moment that in the realm of the unconscious a minotaur is standing guard over our psychic pain. In this case, the interpretation of our dreams is the thread that walks us out of the maze of the unconscious to find ourself at the other end.

TALKING TO YOUR DREAM

The fact that knowledge is derived from experience necessitates that we must not merely watch our dreams, as this makes us passive observers. We must actively participate in our dreams, for there is experience to be gained. We must talk to our dreams (while in the process of dreaming) by questioning the strangeness of their symbols and images. If we see a room in our dreams we must remember that this is a symbol of ourselves. What color did we paint the walls? We must scan the room for clues, for details about how we have decorated the elusive and reclusive unconscious, our inner selves.

Because, if repression is lifted, direct and immediate experience follows. For things are felt and not thought, and reality is *lived* and not *filed away*. Therefore, we must actively seek out our unconscious minds, for there is so much to be learned; for example, we should be able to act in ways that are not contrary to our nature. Unearthing repressed material is learning our unconscious.

AN EXAMPLE OF REPRESSED MATERIAL IN A DREAM WORK

A former patient had the following dream when she was in her late sixties:

I was in my living room and I was re-decorating. I had some powder blue print couches. I noticed I had something I was ready to throw out (like garbage). I open my door and there is a foreign woman at the door and she's talking in a peculiar voice as if she is faking her accent. I think she's a con artist. Somehow she walks into my apartment and she is looking around. I tell her, "you cannot stay here; you do not belong here, you have to get out." I cried out, "mother, mother," but my mother must have been sleeping because she didn't come to my aid. I finally get rid of the woman, and I look through the peephole to make sure that she is no longer there. I don't see her so I throw out the garbage.

When the dreamer was seventeen years of age, she was suspicious of her father's many absences from the home and had followed him to the Plaza Hotel. She watched him walk into a strange room. She stood outside the door and listened. After hearing a strange woman's voice and some of the conversation her suspicions were validated. With a racing heart she managed to knock upon the door, announce herself, and bring her father outside, his face whitened. After a moment of silence her father took her for a walk and spoke apologetically about his infidelity to her mother, and about the other woman, named Constance, inside the room.

The dreamer became an accomplice to her father's dishonesty and betrayal by promising him that she would not tell her mother what she had seen and heard, for her father had promised to inform his wife of the whole matter in his own words the following week; he also noted that he would be divorcing and remarrying in short order.

The traumas of that day—the dreamer's anger, her guilt over her complicity in an unacceptable situation, and most important her sense of powerlessness—all seem to have been repressed, for there was so much to repress: the anger over her father's infidelity, his dishonesty and ultimate betrayal, and the anger she felt over her mother's ignorance of the situation, which had brought about the dreamer's involvement in a veritable sting operation. All the anger melted away under the heat of expensive furs and the tropical sun of the many luxurious vacations paid for by her father. In later years, the repression manifested itself in sporadic bouts of nervousness and anxiety, heart palpitations, and an occasional facial tick.

Then, after all those years, the dreamer had an epiphany. She had reached a resolution—for the above dream clearly shows the return of the repressed, as the statement within the dream notes, "I had something I was ready to throw out." For that which was thrown out came from the dreamer's living room (her mind) as she was redecorating—getting rid of all that was repressed in her unconscious (her guilt, her anger, her sense of being betrayed).

The foreign woman at the door is the *other* woman, *Constance* (which is why she is perceived as a *con* artist). Symbolizing the sudden disruption of the dreamer's life, the other woman "somehow walked into (her) apartment." The dreamer allows herself the long-awaited resolution and vindication as she angrily and authoritatively cries "you don't belong here—you have to get out." The dreamer cries out for her mother who "must have been sleeping" as a reprimand—a manifestation of the original anger the dreamer felt toward her mother for having let her down . . . for not having come to her aid—for having made the dreamer (instead of her mother) confront her father.

Upon examination of the "powder blue *print* couches" that literally left their *imprint* in the dreamer's unconscious, it must be noted that the dreamer was in the habit of wearing powder blue eye shadow to the exclusion of any other color. It is most probable, therefore, that the powder blue of the couch (where couch means to hide or camouflage) is a symbol of the eye shadow worn by the dreamer—which has the phonetic meaning of *I shadow*—and refers to the actual event, of the dreamer following, or *shadowing,* her father to the Plaza Hotel on that fateful day.

When the dreamer finally "gets rid of the woman," she finds her long-awaited resolution, and ends her sense of powerlessness. The woman (who in reality is long since dead) is no longer there. The garbage (the repressed material) is effectively and metaphorically thrown out.

The dream, once interpreted, had the beneficent effect of allowing the dreamer to feel unburdened and at peace. Her facial tick miraculously disappeared.

2

Self-Empowerment

S peaking about gaining self-empowerment through the interpretation of dreams, one need only look at the Bible to find the ultimate example of becoming empowered: According to the Old Testament, Joseph made the transition from impoverished and imprisoned slave boy to regent of the pharaoh because of his skills at interpreting the meanings of dreams. But all Joseph did was to make a fairly obvious *appraisal* of the dream symbols and then use the information in the dream as a *coping response*. In that Joseph's appraisal was a sensible one, the information he imparted came to pass. Joseph could make this interpretive judgment because he fully understood his universe. His conception of the world around him came from the fact that *he knew himself,* and in his self-knowledge was his power. The answer to how one becomes self-empowered is an easy one: *Know thyself.* But this is no easy matter.

KNOW THYSELF

There is no more effective way to gain information about the self than through the analysis of dreams, as dreams are a direct pathway to the unconscious. The more self-information, the larger the self-concept. Individuals with enlarged self-concepts are better equipped at handling adverse environmental or emotional situations and stressors. Knowing oneself enhances self-esteem, which increases levels of self-efficacy. Thus, defining the dream narrative makes it easier to pursue a particular course of action—to reap what one wants to get out of life because one is no longer in doubt or in conflict. This sounds simplistic but it is not. Walking around without understanding one's unconscious is like walking around with a deficit.

DREAM APPRAISAL AS COPING RESPONSE

The interpreting of dreams is a coping strategy—mastery occurs when the coping strategy is adequate enough to resolve the stressors of daily life. Dream analysis done independently, outside of the therapeutic situation (the psychoanalyst's office) can be effective in eliminating stress and enhancing functioning; however, there is more to be gained. This way, the dreamer feels responsible rather than helpless—active rather than passive—and this is the true value of self-help. Autonomy (independence) is perceived, which is in itself self-empowering. One becomes master of one's domain by learning how to open the door—*and by being in possession of the key.* The key is the understanding of one's dreams.

Self-Appraisal and Behavior Modification

• **The positive side effects of having a good dream:** hopefulness, high degree of arousal, high self-esteem or self-affirmation, invigoration, clearheadedness, determination to begin a new day, feelings of peace and serenity.

• **The negative side effects of having a bad dream or nightmare:** low energy level or perceived feeling of weakness (as result of rapid heart beat and/or cold sweat during dream), feelings of insecurity, inadequacy, jealousy, and/or paranoia, guilt, low self-esteem, fearfulness, general feelings of unshakable anxiety and edginess. But let the truth be known—*as long as dreams are understood there are no bad dreams.*

• **Behavior Modification:** Dreams have been known to modify behavior. (See dream of John Waite, who, after his dream, makes the conscious decision to become a vegetarian.) Dreams have stopped dreamers from smoking as the result of troubling symbolism that involves matters of health. Personal realizations attained in dreams have been known to be deciding factors in preventing marriages from ending in divorce. Such behavior modification, when perceived as being positive to the individual, is yet another manifestation of self-empowerment through dreams.

MINIMALIZING CONSCIOUS CONSTRAINTS

There are so many conscious constraints existing in everyday reality that we are all mummies wrapped in our restraining cloths! It is believed that the function of the unconscious is to reduce the tension created by these constraints by enabling the dreamer to express sexual and aggressive impulses in disguised manner, which is what happens in the dreamworld. This is well and good, but once the world of consciousness forgets these highly distorted and sometimes unrecognizable wishful impulses, they serve no purpose other than weighing down the individual dreamer with the energy imposed by repression. Explication minimal-

izes energy spent. *Interpretation is an unwinding process.*
Without allowing our dreams to unwind we remain mummi-
fied—*preserved in the gauze of distortion.* What is sought is
the empowerment that comes from *unwrapping,* as this is
what brings the dreamer into view. Accurate dream interpretation brings an understanding of motivation and desire—
and a position of predictability that allows the dreamer to
influence outcomes.

WARDING OFF STRESS

*Stress is a tacit agreement between the individual and the
stressors* where the individual says—''I will let you bother
me.'' It is an accepted arrangement where the environment
intrudes upon and interacts (or messes) with one's internal
emotional psyche. *It is a reciprocal agreement.* But, instead
of holding the passive belief that the environment influences
the individual, the individual should view him or herself as
actively influencing the environment. For example, in cases
of bereavement the individual has a bevy of feelings to ward
off: feelings of yearning and despair, loneliness and helplessness, betrayal, anger, and guilt. People grieving often have
visitation dreams where they meet the recently deceased
again. Visitation dreams should be viewed as *active tools in
coping* as they help dreamers accept their loss. This is the
dream that allows words to be spoken that were left unsaid—
and reparations to be made. This is an example of how a
dream can change one's psychological landscape. But we
have all too often closed our mental telescopes.

A DISTURBANCE IN THE FORCE

It is thought that many *physiological disturbances* are unconscious displacements. Physiological disturbances are viewed as symbolic expressions of repressed instinctual drives. According to Freud, a symptom is a form of symbolic communication that expresses some wish or impulse in disguised form—because its actual expression is blocked from surfacing. *I suggest that the entire dream is a symptom.* And as a symptom, the old adage applies: *If you want to be healed you must uncover your wound.*

The symptom reflects the disease. The dream is a measure of our *dis-ease,* which must be revealed and treated. Interpretation is the only treatment that gets to the source.

DREAM INTERPRETATION AS IMMUNOLOGY

Immunology is the study of how the body protects and monitors itself from outside invasive forces. (The whole gregarious world in which we interact may be viewed as an external invasive force.)

A relationship exists between the immune system and events that occur in the unconscious. The brain and specifically the unconscious dream play a role in moderating immune status. Stress comes from not being able to handle an experience or stressors, from not understanding or being able to disarm a negative experience. In that stress has been known to alter the body's immune response, it would be worthwhile to study the physiological aftereffects of a bad dream. We already know there is change in heart rate and blood pressure, but do we know if dreamers fall sick after a particularly distressing dream? Answering this question is well beyond the scope of this book; I can only suggest the reasonableness of this research. Dreams are mediators between unconsciousness and cognitive awareness. Not understanding dreams brings feelings of loss of control to dreamers and often elicits feelings of depression. Understanding dreams has the empowering potential of eliminating neurotic conflicts, relieving stress, and strengthening our immune systems.

REGARDING SUPERMAN

The kryptonite of consciousness causes the death of the unconscious dream. How relevant is it that the metaphorical kryptonite is a syllogism of two Greek words that form to mean "secret night"—and how frightening is it to learn that the only way to destroy Superman is through the element of kryptonite. The English word *cryptic* signifies that which is encoded. Thus, what is encoded can harm us and render us powerless.

We know from the comic strip that exposure to kryptonite means death for Superman—he weakens until the last of his strength is relinquished and he dies. He loses his powers through a metaphorical element that is much like an unanalyzed cryptic dream of the night. We must use our interpretative abilities to decode our dreams of the night, for we owe the superman in all of us his right to live.

GIVING VOICE TO THE UNCONSCIOUS

Freud has compared dream interpretation to the decoding of hieroglyphics or to the solution of a rebus, because the dream cannot speak; he goes on to say that instead of speaking *it dreams*. But there is a way to turn this mute performer into a world-class tenor or soprano—a way to give voice to the unconscious—and that is by *listening*. Listening and then taking responsibility, for the dreamer is responsible for the dream.

The dream is a manifestation of symbolic human action—an action that may be interpreted as directed and purposeful. And like conscious human actions there is an *intentionality* to whatever actions are taken and, thus, a responsibility. However, how is one to assume responsibility for one's dreams when unconscious motives remain out of view (repressed) as the basis underlying conscious actions? During the dream this hidden agenda takes refuge in the form of *displacement* (substitution), *condensation* (combination), *representation* (the use of symbolism and imagery, particularly the use of metaphor—when something is something else or is substituted for something else), and *secondary revision* (perception of waking thoughts). How does one get through these elements of distortion?

The benefit of interpreting the dream is that whatever has been repressed can be recovered (unearthed), brushed off, and viewed in its entirety. In other words, that which has been repressed must be analyzed in relation to current life circumstances. A failure to interpret or *translate* a dream is to buy into repression. Repression disallows creative spontaneity, which finds its expressive outlet in the unconscious symbol. The purpose of interpretation is that it opens up the unconscious and allows the dreamer to discourse and fantasize about unconscious representations, metaphors, symbols, and images.

Though the dream is written down it is still mum, speechless. Giving voice to the dream means elaborating on the images. In no uncertain terms this means that the dreamer should go beyond the dream narrative and try to fantasize either an ending to the dream or try to visualize an un-recognizable *(or undiagnosed)* image or symbol as something else. These fantasies of the conscious imagination may be more helpful than the remembered nocturnal narrative because they are *imagined* by a conscious mind rather than an unconscious one. And imagining is free, uninhibited, unrestrained thinking that is parallel to the thinking of the unconscious mind. Yet being conscious, there is no need for disguise, because the dreamer *wants to know,* is applying him or herself *to know,* if for no other reason than that of curiosity. It is this imagining, which comes so easily to children and yet is perceived as such a difficult task for adults, that expands consciousness. And through this expansion comes self-empowerment.

EXPRESS YOUR DREAM

The dreamer must review the dream from an emotional stance and define how he or she feels it. Focus should be placed on any anxiety-producing problem or conflict within the dream until a solution is reached. For the dream may often indicate the dreamer's way of reacting to the world and to problems of conflict, in particular, as in flying dreams wherein the wish is to rise above one's troubles. By expressing one's emotions a cognitive perspective can be reached. But as a dream often represents a distortion of reality a maladaptive appraisal can lead to a faulty cognition. This is because anxiety is often free-floating and hard to pin down. Because anxiety is often of nondeterminate origin, the anxiety within the dream should be linked to a current anxiety, for once the anxiety is recognized *it can be modified!*

The dream, if perceived correctly, will in every instance be seen as a cognitive intervention.

THE BENEFIT OF FANTASIES

To the extent that a dream is temporarily experienced as a reality, the fantasy within that dream is momentarily perceived as a reality. Thus, upon waking, dreamers should be encouraged to continue these fantasies so that they are seen and felt—both intellectually and emotionally—during consciousness. This is *induced dreaming* or what I call *indirect dreaming*.

Apart from the dream, the usefulness of this type of visualization or fantasy technique is that it enables behavior modification. It has been found to enhance learning or motor skills—from general performance functioning and public speaking to having a better tennis serve. Such observances suggest that fantasies contribute to achieving skills that, in turn, heighten one's sense of self-worth, acceptance, competence, and control, which has as its by-product the overcoming of anxiety in daily life situations. It is unfortunate that individuals with a negative self-image fear that their lack of competence will prevent them from mastering problematic situations and reaching their goals—for the very fear perpetuates the negative outcome. Thus, the benefit of induced or indirect dreaming is that it propels these individuals into confronting their fears or negative assumptions.

Indirect dreaming is defined as the visual elaboration of the dream narrative during consciousness, for this conscious and thus directed elaboration will help the dreamer alter certain negative fantasies by allowing the dreamer to be distanced from his or her anxiety. The dreamer is now the narrator, the one telling the story.

UNDERSTANDING AND COMBATING VULNERABILITY

A nightmare or even a typical anxiety dream that has not been properly interpreted can provoke feelings of vulnerability in the dreamer, where vulnerability is defined as the perception that one is subject to dangers one has no control over or chance of overcoming—where one's sense of personal safety has been tampered with. The coping strategies of the dream, having failed, have left the dreamer filled with the sense of dread, of uncertainty and ambiguity.

Being a passive observer to your own bad dream means that you do not react aggressively, so there is little chance to bolster your self-image or discharge anxiety or anger. Not knowing or being able to decipher what you are dreaming leads to a sense of the elusiveness of information and therefore frustration; there is the feeling of lack of accomplishment and uselessness of effort. And although aware *(because of the bad dream's absence of approval, praise, or appreciation)* that you *have* inner conflicts, they remain undiagnosed and unrectified.

Often the anxiety produced by a bad dream is reflective of a poor self-image. Often dreamers tend to think that a bad dream means they are under stress. In one particular recurring dream the dreamer arrives at work and is unable to turn on the lights. When he finally solves that problem something else gets shorted out so that he cannot effect a change or control his situation. The dreamer's stress increases to the degree of the depreciation of his sense of self. (Feeling incompetent is definitely a stressor.) Having a negative self-concept leads to behavior consistent with that belief. This is an example of cognitive misperception. The actual dream was one in which the dreamer creatively solved a problem only to be challenged with another one. The image of turning on the light puts a positive skew on the dreamer—he is searching for elucidation and clarity. A correct interpretation of the dream would have been constructive in that it would have served as a check against negative views—the image of being weak or ineffectual. Therefore, it is important to note that anxiety, in most dreams, is an extension of problems that the dreamer is facing in his or her current situation, but, more important, it is also a statement about *how* the dreamer deals with and conceptualizes the problem. How you deal with your problem is related to the way you have dealt with problems throughout your life and is thus, self-revelatory. Knowing who you are is a major step in combating vulnerability by reestablishing control—for those in control are empowered.

OVERCOMING ANXIETY

Anxiety is like stage fright in that it happens behind a closed curtain. It can therefore be thought of as a *pre-event* in that preperformance jitters usually calm during the actual performing. The more performances, the more experience one has in handling this form of anxiety that comes from being *exposed* before the scrutinizing eye of the audience. The more one is exposed, the less one has to hide. The less one has to hide, the more accessible the information; the more probable the outcome, the less anxious the player and the less anxious the audience. *What is needed is exposure.*

The dream is the player and the audience all in one. But

the dream is also the publicist who will get *one's uncon- scious* exposure, for the dream places the dreamers on the stage of the unconscious so their stories may be told.

For anxiety must be played. But in order to be meaning- fully played one must know the motivation behind the char- acter's (dreamer's) actions, the behavioral quirks, the attitudinal responses. This is done by reading the narrative text (of the dreams), by studying the dialogue, and by inter- preting the symbolic content. More important, the character must be experienced, for only through experience will the dreamers be aware of what they can *expect* from their dream characters—the limitations, the attributes. This expectation, however, bears striking similarity to the anxiety-ridden neu- rotic's concern over outcomes or probabilities. This brings us to the realization of why the dream—the publicist—is in such demand. For being exposed has everything to do with the predictability of outcome, the extinguisher of anxiety.

3

How to Remember Your Dream

As the birth of dreams, their evolution, formulation, nurturing, and maturation all occur in the realm of the unconscious, dreams learn to communicate in the visual language of their derivation—in symbols and images—which is why they are fully understood and remembered by the unconscious dreaming mind. Wonderful! This is why the dreamer has no deciphering or memory problem *while asleep* . . . because the dreams are not *foreigners,* but rather *citizens by inception.* And as a dreamer in the realm of the unconscious, the dreamer is a citizen as well. The dreamer speaks the language, knows the grammar.

But, upon awakening, dream recall is made difficult by our lack of translation skills. This is precisely because, when awake, we are all *immigrants* who have migrated back to our understandable world of consciousness where we are subjected once again to the daily demands of everyday living and the surrounding stimuli of the senses, particularly the intrusive sights, sounds, feelings, and smells that serve as distractions. Necessarily, as conscious migrants we begin thinking of the day ahead, of plans, worries, anxieties, and ideas, for we are now awake and thinking in the mindset of consciousness, communicating and receiving input in the vocabulary of the conscious mind that we understand so well.

Our masterful ego is in control again, ever watchful and protective, ready to repress any uncomfortable thought at the blink of an eye. But, repression aside, herein lies the real reasons we forget our dreams: *Upon awakening we are no longer dreamers, we are no longer unconscious, and we are no longer part of this other unconscious country that communicates through the semantics of the dream idiom*—we no longer speak or understand how to translate the dream vocabulary.

There is a wonderful *Seinfeld* episode where Jerry awakens from a dream laughing hysterically. He scribbles down what he thinks is hilarious only to find upon awakening in the morning that whatever his unconscious had found so amusing the night before had lost all traces of humor. His unconscious got it, but consciously, much to his consternation, he is not even close to smiling. . . . He might just as well be in a comedy club in Africa listening to a tribesman comedian telling jokes in Swahili.

Therefore, in order to remember our dreams upon awakening, it is imperative to remain, for as long as possible, *conscious in the world of the unconscious.* No easy trick, this. For to master this feat we must practice lying perfectly still, not moving a muscle, and not opening our eyes, as this not only limits the commands that the brain sends by way of neural transmissions to the moving of our limbs, but also makes minimal the amount of exposure to the distracting stimuli of the conscious world. For only in this feigned paralytic state may we dreamers begin to mull over our dream, to try to remain *in* it, and *with* it, to recap the action, to view the dream cinematically as a movie we have just seen. Then, and only then, must we rapidly jot down these very thoughts and images on that piece of paper we have cleverly left near our beds specifically for this purpose. Once we have written down the basic script of the dream we may add any accompanying remarks or associations (see Appendix).

BASIC STEPS

1. Before going to sleep a pen and paper, at the very least, must be placed by your bed. The pen may be replaced by a tape recorder. The paper may be replaced with a blank-paged notebook exclusively for the recording of your dreams, although a ruled notebook with vertical margins drawn down the left side of each page is preferable.

2. Remember to date your paper or notebook.

3. Tell yourself that you are going to dream. Declare this aloud.

4. Upon awakening, do not move a muscle. Lie perfectly still with your eyes closed. Ask yourself what you were thinking. Remain with what is happening in the dream. Stay with it. Finish it if you want. But do not allow any other thoughts to enter into your consciousness.

5. When you feel you remember the gist of the dream, do not get out of bed, but rather reach slowly for the pen and paper, and record immediately, even in a scribble, whatever you remember of your dream in as much detail as possible. Set down whatever comes into your mind first, no matter how trivial it seems . . . even a dream fragment. Do not try to recall the full dream, or necessarily the correct order.

6. Be aware of any personal, experiential associations to your dream images, and jot these down in the margin alongside the dream text. For example: You just dreamt of exiting a building. You remember that the previous day you had been strolling the streets of Manhattan's Lower East Side and had made a mental note of all the antiquated fire escapes attached to the exterior walls of old buildings. As it is not far-fetched to accept that your stroll from the other day may have contributed to a dream wherein you were concerned with fleeing your apartment, this memory must be written down, as it may lead you to a more profound association. You now realize that the viewing of this image happens to coincide to a time in your life when you are contemplating ending a difficult personal relationship. At this point you will recognize the emotional relevance and significance of your dream symbolization.

7. Focus on colors, the time of day, the season, clothing, surroundings (are you inside or outside?), placement of objects or people: right or left, up or down, under or above, behind or in front. Focus on dialogue and write it down using quotation marks. Try to remember exactly the way something was said.

8. If your dream has occurred in the middle of the night, number it Dream #1, write it down, and go back to sleep. Multiple dreams should be ordered consecutively. Any new dreams should be transcribed in the same manner the next morning.

9. After all of the above, reread what you have written and add more associations as they come to mind. Most important, you must be aware of how the dream has made you feel upon awakening in order to define your emotional state. Are you feeling happy, sad, angry, jittery, guilty, jealous, frustrated, or at peace. Write down how you feel.

10. Now try to relate your dream to the day residue, the

events of the previous day that may have triggered the dream.

11. Try to categorize the type dream you have had. (See The Nine Types of Dreams.)

12. Lastly, try to categorize your dream into one of the thirty-three dream motifs.

PART II

**Sweet
Dreams
Are
Made
of
This...**

DEFINING YOUR DREAM

The Nine Types of Dreams

- *The Anxiety Dream*
- *The Traumatic Anxiety Dream*
- *The Self-Affirmation Dream*
- *The Wish-Fulfillment Dream*
- *The Oedipal or Libidinous Dream*
- *The Problem-Solving Dream*
- *The Examination Dream*
- *The Initiation Dream*
- *The Prophetic Dream*

4

The Anxiety Dream

The anxiety dream may be viewed as a product of our having to live in what social scientists have previously termed the age of anxiety, presently thought of as the age of stress. These dreams evoke the unnerved image of Woody Allen wringing his hands in angst in that they anticipate the daily problematic annoyances of waking life and all the dangers we are heir to. They thrive on our fears, frustrations, worries, and conflicts, and on our imagined inability to cope. Because most anxiety dreams occur whenever we feel overwhelmed or at a loss, we may say that they focus on our *insecurities* rather than our strengths, while holding us in the grip of the most dreadful situations or feelings. Yet, as opposed to being reflective, these dreams dwell on the future, on the *what-ifs*.

As anxiety dreams nail down the stressful realization that we are not in control of our lives, they tend to elicit subject matter that is of chaotic and even nightmarish proportions, for something clearly unpleasant and disagreeable is occurring. With our intentions either frustrated, thwarted, or misunderstood, the editing of these dreams is usually haphazard and frenzied—the cinematic mood is one of hopelessness and dread. Dreams that include *forgetting, losing,* or *disorienting* motifs, or narrations where we are ourselves lost, are also anxiety producing although the anxiety often resolves itself before the end of the dream.

The most significant feature of an anxiety dream is that the anxiety never ceases or is never resolved during the course of the dream, such that the dreamer often awakens in a sweat, feeling unnerved and on edge. Examine the following dream of prima ballerina and academy-award-winning actress, **Leslie Browne,** as it is an anxiety dream par excellence:

> *I was being chased, trying to run away but these bright lights were in front of me, blinding me, like headlights, preventing me from knowing where I was going, so I couldn't get away. I was terrified of the bright lights.*

This recurring childhood dream reveals Leslie's anxiety about her future—about the direction in which her life is headed. Thus, within the dream Leslie tries to view what is ahead of her, the future. But her attempt is thwarted as she is blinded by the lights. The bright lights may symbolize the sun dawning on the horizon, and as dawn usually *precedes* the completion of an unfinished work, there is more work to be done. The task at hand is to reveal the dark recesses of the unconscious mind, which is why the dreamer is terrified of the lights—and what they will expose.

Whereas darkness usually represents ambivalence, chaos, or what is lacking in illumination, light always refers to consciousness and awareness. In that light is usually a positive symbol that represents a higher understanding and clarity, it is most unusual for it to be equated with fear. As we shall see, perhaps light must be shed on a situation that would be better left in the shadows. But the fear element associated with the blinding lights does not disguise the fact that the wish of the dream is for illumination and enlightenment. Leslie can no longer avoid the unseen depths of her unconscious desires. If the light that is feared represents the light at the end of the tunnel, imagine the despair that exists within the tunnel.

As bright lights symbolize success, being "terrified of the bright lights" signifies Leslie's deep fear of accomplishment and notoriety. It seems that fame has had a negative effect—it has gotten in Leslie's way because it has *gone to her head,* via the symbolic headlights. The lights are viewed as detractors. With the lights in front of Leslie, she alarmingly casts no shadow, her essence is blotted out, her features are flattened. This indicates that the dreamer has lost substance and her sense of identity, in the process . . . which is a steep price to pay for fame. The dreamer, blinded by the lights, has lost her way. She is terrified that she has veered from the virtuous path of the straight and narrow, as being chased has the phonetic rendering of being *chaste,* or morally pure. The dream reveals Leslie's anxiety about her lifestyle and is an admission of the seductiveness of fame. The dream has no resolution but instead has the effect of making the dreamer aware of the value of keeping a low profile.

The following anxiety dream of **Allen Ginsberg**'s was dreamt on January 19, 1995, nearly two years before his death, and was entitled "Bardo," because he believed the dream revealed that he had fully accepted the passive Buddhist tenet of fearlessly easing into the chaos of space that exists between life and death. Thus, Mr. Ginsberg thought he would be going gently into that long good night. However, after receiving and analyzing the dream six months before Mr. Ginsberg's death, it seems that, as the dream was filled with fears of death, he was embroiled in passion and fire, with the steadfast determination *not* to go gently but rather *fiercely* into that last good-night sleep.

> *I was in a foreign city like Paris, London, Milan, —*
> *Time to board the plane for home — We were in the*
> *passenger terminal going thru customs inspection, pa-*
> *pers to be shown — Panicked suddenly and realized*
> *didn't have my ticket, or passport, I'd left them home*
> *— My companion a young lady, mature, relatively*
> *friendly acquaintance who was also going on same*
> *plane — "What time is it?" I wondered, didn't see my*
> *watch? "It's 2:30" — she answered. "And when does*
> *the plane leave?" "It's at 10" — "So we have till 10*
> *to get home, get my papers — and my baggage to*
> *travel!! But is it that it's 10 A.M. & we leave at 2:30 or*
> *is it 10 P.M. or is it 2:30 P.M. & we leave at 10 P.M. or 10*
> *A.M.? — I got confused . . . I can't think straight" I*
> *say, and realize something's wrong with my calcula-*
> *tion & hope she can think it thru & calculate it. Did she*
> *say it was 2:30 A.M. or P.M. or 10 P.M.? Do I have a*
> *couple hours to get my baggage? We're outside, driv-*
> *ing in her car, but now I can't remember where my*
> *hotel is, something's wrong with me — Is it Hotel La-*
> *tour-Mauberg? No it's not Paris — Where are we?*
> *What city? . . . I settle down in front seat. She's driv-*
> *ing thank god but where, she asks me again, Where's*
> *my hotel? "I don't know, don't remember." I realize*
> *what's happened, "I think I've had a stroke . . . I*
> *don't remember the last days . . . I don't know*
> *where I am or where my hotel is, I must have had a*
> *stroke," I tell her, thinking this must be stroke aphasia.*
> *If I say "I had a stroke" maybe this lady will take it*
> *seriously & get help for me, get me to some help —*
> *She's a casual acquaintance, I couldn't count on much*

attention from her but this seems serious & I remember
I'm famous enough that someone will take an interest
in my plight and make an effort to locate my last resi-
dence & get me home where I can be taken care of.

The above dream is laden with anxiety caused by a dreamer's forgetfulness at crucial moments, which thwart his efforts to return home. Because forgetting involves the disappearance of the power of selection and efficiency, it is plausible to assume that the dreamer has cleverly *used* forgetting as it serves his purpose and allays his angst. As the disguised wish of the dream is to forestall the journey, the dreamer *must* forget his ticket, as his forgetfulness lets him avoid what he fears most, the departure, a metaphor for death.

Control is deflected to the dreamer's companion who is "driving in her car." The companion is viewed as a mother substitute because the dreamer is *not* in the driver's seat but rather "settled down in front," as though he is being carried in his mother's stomach. Also, in the phrase "relatively friendly acquaintance," the word *relatively* insures the familial relationship. In keeping with the fetal metaphor the dreamer is totally dependent on his companion. Having lost his sense of autonomy—his powers of judgment and inference—Ginsberg cannot remember the location or name of his hotel and therefore should not be able to make the following assessment of his mental state. Yet, he theorizes that his lack of orientation must be a symptom of stroke aphasia.

When a symptom is diagnosed *within* a dream it suggests that an ongoing analysis is being conducted by the dreamer. This reflects the analytic nature of Mr. Ginsberg but also siphons back the control that Mr. Ginsberg gives away when he allocates his calculating faculties to his companion—

which means that he vacillates between the desire of losing control and the wish for gaining it back again. Similarly, there is vacillation between anxiety and tranquillity as the dreamer unbelievably settles down in the front seat after his frantic cry, "Where are we? What city?"—as "settles down" is associated with calmness. But as we shall see "settles down" has another physiological implication.

In a metaphorical sense, foreign city, and passenger terminal are perceived as womb symbols. Being in both places strongly indicates that the dreamer wishes to return to his mother's womb. Strengthening this view, there is also the pregnancy symbolism of being "settled down in the front seat" of his companion's car. The passport that was left at home literally means that there will be no passing from this port. Thus, "the pass port" is the birth canal that the dreamer wants to avoid—for his wish is to stay within the womb. By wishing for rebirth the possibility of death is eliminated and a death fear is overcome. The companion, "mature and relatively friendly," is the rescuer, which in dreams means the one who births, the mother. She is the driver—the *vehicle* that will get the dreamer "home where he can be taken care of" in motherly fashion. The dreamer consoles himself that "an effort will be made to locate his last residence." This is the cunning wish of the dreamer to return to the safety of the womb (to avoid death) and to await eventual rebirth.

The following dream remembrance of **Avery Fisher,** the founder of Fisher Radio and the man who endowed Avery Fisher Hall, expresses anxiety over the work situation. Avery Fisher's son, Chip Fisher, recalls his father's dream:

He often dreamt that little "source pixies" would come in and rob his mind of ideas that made his equip-

ment aesthetically special. They would ask him questions. He was afraid he would give them the source, and so he would wake up in a cold sweat.

Although he worked in an *auditory* world manufacturing radios, Mr. Fisher was a *visionary* who prided himself on his meticulous attention to details. Even throughout the post–war years when materials were scarce Mr. Fisher knew just where to find them, often traveling through war-torn countries for the best chassis or the most "aesthetically special" jewel-colored lights. It is no surprise, therefore, that Fisher dreams of having his company secrets stolen by competitors, who are symbolized as "source pixies." Yet, on a deeper level the dream takes on philosophical significance.

As radios are communicating devices, Avery may have imaginatively likened his mind to a radio that freely transmits thoughts and gives away information, such as "sources," over the air to anyone listening. In that the mind is the source of the human being that determines its uniqueness and capacity to be "aesthetically special," the mind's ideas must be guarded. If questioned, the dreamer would answer truthfully, give up source information crucial to his essence. The fact that Mr. Fisher awakens indicates the extent of his anxiety and the value placed on inspirational thought.

There is another type of anxiety dream—the performance anxiety dream—wherein dreamers are stressed about their capacity to perform a function to the best of their abilities. The following was dreamt by a young lawyer:

My little dog, who looked curiously like a squirrel in the dream, was beneath a countertop on which many carrots were being chopped into small pieces. I hear a

*drum roll. Then, one by one the pieces of carrots are
thrown so that the dog can demonstrate how well he
fetches.*

The dream depicts a small dog that has to perform. In that
this is the dreamer's dog it is safe to assume that the dog
represents the dreamer himself. The dog, that is visualized as
a squirrel, conjures up an image of a rodent squirreling away
acorns for a rainy day—and signifies that security is an issue.
Here, what is saved, salvaged, or worked for are carrots,
symbolic of money or wages. "Carrots" in its obscure reference to the worth and weight of gold symbolizes what is
saved, salvaged or worked for. Carrots may also represent
clients . . . The young lawyer is "thrown" a new client to
represent.

The little dog, who is beneath the countertop, is literally
the underdog, the newcomer, the small fish in the big sea.
The drum roll signals that an audience is watching in antici-
pation. A performance is about to begin. The carrots being
portioned out and thrown signify the work assignments given
to the young lawyer—*he is thrown a bone;* he must do the
fetching or someone else's bidding, and he must perform
well because the partners are watching. Thus, the pressure
and anxiety of work has found its outlet in the dreamworld.
For, in this *dog-eat-dog* world we live in, the dreamer is able
to reduce some of his stress by envisioning himself as his
own dog and by becoming his own best friend.

Beyond the typical anxiety dream is a specific *anxiety-
revealing* dream that signals depression. In these dreams the
dreamers are struck with the sense of impending doom.
Things happen forcefully and unaccountably as the dreamer
feels a loss of control, an unstable and disharmonious pres-

ence of mind. Windows symbolizing the mind or the psyche often appear as broken—glass is shattered, explosions go off. The following anxiety dream of **Esther Levy,** foreign correspondent of *Marie Claire* magazine, is typical of the sort of dreams that are often dreamt during periods of depression, wherein the dreamers turn more introspective:

> *An earthquake, a hurricane, many disasters are happening in New York City. The sky is very grey. I am in my bedroom which has two windows, one in front of me and the other behind me behind my bed. Through the front window I see the buildings are falling like dominoes falling towards me. I look behind at my back window to see if it looks shaky outside. If it looks safe I will leave through the back window but there is water behind me and it is shaky as well. My room starts shaking. My younger sister gets up panicky and I smile at her very peacefully.*

The visual landscape of the above dream is crumbling, falling to pieces. The dreamer is coming undone. As the room is the dreamer, the problem (coming from outside the room) is external to the dreamer and situationally induced—"the sky is very grey." Something is hanging like a shroud—the overcast sky has blotted out the sun (where "sun" could symbolize son and thus by reversal symbolize daughter). The disasters, earthquakes, and hurricanes are not man-made but rather caused by Mother Nature—a controlling force. The bedroom with its two windows signifies that the dreamer is being watched over by parental eyes.

Esther's view of what is in front of her (the future) is just as grim as where she has come from—what is behind her (the past). Yet, the dreamer links the past with the future in an effort to preserve an inward understanding of the whole. In other words, the unconscious is aware of a shaky past but anticipates even greater problems in the future. The buildings "falling like dominoes" are detaching themselves, wherein this symbolic detachment becomes the threat of the outside world—of leaving the home (or mother). In other words, leaving the home incorporates the disguised wish to stay connected with the mother in that what is outside is perceived as threatening. The falling buildings are symbolic of a frontal assault on the dreamer to make her aware that her space is being invaded.

But the question remains: Is this dream a wish for survival or emancipation? For the dreamer is able to "smile peacefully" in the face of adversity, as though in a kind of protest to the dereliction of nature. The smile is the force of reason and intellect against the physical powers of nature—against an unreasonable power. By smiling at her younger sister the dreamer assumes the role of the mother and thus survives— as *Mother* Nature is the ruling force. Unconsciously viewing herself as responsible empowers the dreamer with a sense of confidence. This is the defensive mechanism of the dream trying to dispel the dreamer's depression over her conflicted fear of and need for attachment.

5

The Traumatic Anxiety Dream

A lthough contrary to what it seems, the traumatic anxiety dream is actually *protective* in nature. It is a recurring dream that utilizes repetition or imitation in a concerted effort to allow learning to take place. It may, therefore, be viewed as a perfect example of Darwin's theory of adaptation, with survival as its goal. Necessarily, the traumatic dream is all about the process of acclimatization, for the repetition of the dream allows the dreamer sufficient time to become adjusted to the traumatic event. The dream seeks through each new repetition to weaken, defuse, or dilute the trauma until it exhausts or rids itself of the energy attached to the trauma. It is a form of inoculation. It is like the theory behind Andy Warhol's 1963 multiple-disaster silk screens, such as *Five Deaths Seventeen Times,* or *White Car Crash Nineteen Times,* that depict the same disaster over and over again in a way that is meant to desensitize or inure the viewer to the pain of the victim . . . to help the emotions form a cool detachment. In other words, as Warhol's silk screens (or the mass media for that matter) reduce dying to a banal occurrence, these traumatic repetition dreams help assimilate the trauma into the general or familiar as opposed to the specific.

Doctors who have witnessed numerous deaths cannot

maintain their first emotional response any more than the callused bare feet of Hindus, having walked hundreds of times over hot coals, can still feel the pain. Because the stimuli at the time of the traumatic event overpower the dreamer, his or her nervous system becomes involved. Thus, the situation must be brought back home at a time when the dreamer is removed from the proximity of the event in an attempt to allow the experience to lose its shock value. The dream tries to minimize feelings of helplessness by maximizing feelings of control. The following is an example of a traumatic anxiety dream dreamt by the comedian **Soupy Sales:**

> *I am in a plane. . . . I'm flying. . . . It's not an easy flight. There is turbulence and the plane is doing a few loops. I am frightened because I think the plane will crash.*

Any experience that evokes distressing symptoms such as fright or anxiety is a trauma to the system. The situation in the above dream was triggered by a traumatic remembrance the dreamer has of World War II, where he actually witnessed a B-42 bomber crashing into an air force base outside of San Diego, exploding and killing the entire crew. But, though the trauma was taken from reality, the dream alters the situation and makes the dreamer actively involved (inside the plane) instead of passively watching from outside. Anxiety in a dream is presented as a repetition of the trauma in a different, diluted, weakened form, in the hope that the dreamer may gain control over the event. For the mind has had too little time to deal with the powerful disturbance of the traumatic experience that suddenly presents itself. Therefore, when the dreamer repeats the fright, he turns away from the experience and changes it. The trauma is repeated in a conscientious and reparative effort on the part of the unconscious to dispose of and master the fright created from the initial experience in a preparatory effort. In other words, should a dangerous situation recur in the future, the dreamer will not succumb to former feelings of physical helplessness.

The dream wishes to master the fearful effects of the original trauma. By redreaming the event the dreamer boldly does battle with the original fright and feeling of helplessness, displaying the self-preservation instinct, in that each new repetition brings with it the consciousness of present safety, the memory of what happened afterwards. The anxiety in the dream, although fully attributable to the stressful real-life experience of the dreamer, can also be related to the turbulence of the dreamer at the moment, for life is never an easy ride and never without its ups and downs, its loops and endless circles. Many times the destination is unclear and the arrival indefinite. At times like these the traumatic anxiety dream will repeat itself.

A former patient of mine had been suffering from traumatic anxiety dreams that related to a past event: a fire that started in the apartment above where he had been living. The dreams were repetitions of that fire. In the dreams the smoke would fill his living room and he would be consumed with the fear that he would not be able to leave his apartment in time; he would try to move toward the door but feel paralyzed to do so. He felt like he was choking or suffocating; he had the claustrophobic feeling that he was unable to breathe and that the walls were closing in on him. He feared that he would die of asphyxiation.

Something as harmless as a fire truck that had passed him by as he walked down the street would frequently serve as the antecedent of his recurring dream. Of greater interest is the fact that his fear was associated with not being able to leave his home rather than with the actual fire—and that the dream would often recur after he had had a dispute in what was an already fired up and combustible relationship. The traumatic anxiety dream allowed the dreamer to come to terms with the real nature of his anxiety—he wanted to terminate his long-term relationship with his girlfriend, but his strong feelings of obligation had made him feel that this was not an option. After this revelation—his emotional and intellectual understanding of the situation—the dream never recurred.

Yet another example of a recurring, traumatic anxiety dream was dreamt by **Heather Cohane,** the publisher of *Quest* magazine. The trauma was induced by environmental conditions. The dream is as follows:

> *Years ago, in England during W.W. II, I had a recurring childhood dream that I was chased by a frog that would frighten me. He'd chase me to the edge of a cliff . . . a precipice, and then I'd wake up.*

With the suspense of a cliffhanger the dreamer is chased to the edge of a cliff—this edge reveals the edginess of the dreamer. Standing on the precipice symbolizes being on the brink of a dangerous situation and reflects the trauma of a child growing up in war-torn England during World War II. The dream signifies Heather's anxiety over the disastrous world condition. Thus, dreaming of being pursued represents the threat of being invaded by the enemy from across the sea—a real and present danger.

The frog is a cold-blooded amphibian that can leap great

distances, from one place to another—from France to England, perhaps. Point of fact: Frogs have historically been the source of superstitions—having been thought to fall from the sky during a rain, much like the blitzkrieg. What better symbol, then, for the enemy on the other side of the sea? Similarly, the men who executed underwater military maneuvers during the war were known as frogmen.

The value of the dream's recurrence is that the dreamer is allowed to give voice and vision to her deepest and perhaps unspoken fears. Identifying and facing whatever one is afraid of in a dream often enables a sense of courage to develop wherein the dreamer is able to regain a certain measure of control.

The following traumatic anxiety dream was dreamt by **Fabrice,** half of the ill-fated, multiplatinum singing sensation Milli Vanilli:

> *I go to an open air club. It's an old stone barn with a big bell. At the entrance they want me to pay, but I say "I don't pay" and "This better be good." I'm in the VIP room when these security guys came running after me with knives and guns because I talked badly about the place. There was not enough happening for me. I was being chased. I ran back to this round valley.*

The old barn in the open air under the stars represents a manger or nativity scene where the big bell tolls for rebirth, resurrection, and forgiveness. By looking for rebirth in an open air club the dreamer is clearly wishing to reestablish his musical career out in the open, for all to see (where nothing can be covered over or faked) in order to be accepted back into the musical fold, so to speak. Yet, the haunting phrase, "they want me to pay," indicates Fabrice's anxiety over the continual need for retribution. Thus, the dream takes a defensive position as Fabrice says, "I don't pay," which really can be read as, "I should not have to pay as I was signed into a flawed agreement with my producer that I was forced to uphold." The dream repeats itself in an attempt to defuse the trauma, as it allows Fabrice to view himself as the martyr or the sacrificial lamb of Milli Vanilli.

In protective fashion, the dream establishes Fabrice's confidence in himself as a talented singer as he positions himself where he belongs—in the VIP room. There is a wish fulfillment in that the somewhat threatening phrase, "this better be good," is said by Fabrice; for this allows him the chance to dole out critical evaluation, as *he* is now the one who judges or evaluates as opposed to being the recipient of outside societal criticism. But the unconscious dream contains the daunting memory of all the anger that was directed at Fabrice, as there are those chasing after him who seek to bring him down with knives and guns. In an explanatory reversal, Fabrice justifies why he has been chased out of the club—because he has spoken badly about the club instead of vice versa.

He runs back to a round valley—a womb symbol—which represents salvation, wholeness, and completeness, with the wish to make things come out all right in the end. In reality, the valley is where Fabrice lives and practices his songs on his four track, happily immersed in the nurturing world of his music, in doing what fulfills him the most—rehearsing his new material.

6

The Self-Affirmation
Dream

Self-affirmation dreams start out with problematic or distressing content, as in typical anxiety dreams, the difference being that we are allowed to surmount whatever difficulty we are in to reestablish a faith in ourselves, in our sense of self. Inspirational and uplifting, they allow us to regain the illusion that we are in consummate control of our lives—that we can do the impossible. These dreams are hand-clappers that never cease to applaud us—voices that sing our praise. Affirmation dreams of this sort frequently include flying motifs, as they often present us with superman skills, supernatural powers, and great strengths: We can leap buildings in a single bound, carry huge weights, move boulders, exist beyond time. Some examples of self-affirmation dreams follow. The first of these dreams is **Mark Hamill**'s:

> I woke up late to get to the theater. I call in to say I'll
> be there a half hour later. Time is of the essence. I run
> down to Columbus Ave. but there are no cabs. Some-
> how I am able to leap into the air in slow motion to the
> height of a second story building. Then I touch down.
> Finally I get to the theater where they're all waiting for
> me, saying "Thank God you've arrived!" I'm hustled

onto the stage. I know what lines I have to say but I'm not sure what play we're doing.

Mark dreamt this self-affirmation dream (which may also be viewed as a typical actor's nightmare) when he had gone home to rest during the break he had between the matinee and evening performance of a previewing musical. Because the director frequently made changes from one performance to the next, Mark often returned to find the play different from his expectation, which accounts for his dream image of being "hustled onto the stage" of life where the outcome is unsure, bewildered by knowing what lines he has to say, but not knowing when or where to use them.

Waking up late throws Mark off course in his appointed rounds and symbolizes a sense of disorientation and uncertainty. But the dream remarkably turns self-doubt into self-affirmation when Mark calls to tell the people waiting for him, "I'll be there," as this indicates his dependability and affirms an inner confidence in himself. Interestingly, by "walking the sky," the dream foreshadows Mark's future Jedi namesake—the *Star Wars* character Luke *Skywalker*—for by sheer will he is able to leap into the air and span great distances. This symbolizes self-affirmation as Mark has come up in the world, and has risen above life's indefiniteness. Making good use of time, he strides like a winner. For even when he touches down, he scores big as he is enthusiastically told by his peers, "you've arrived"—an expression that conveys a high position in life. Thus, the original anxiety of the dream has been thwarted by the dreamer's resourcefulness: against all odds he can be depended upon.

Even though the action around Mark is unstable and unpredictable, it does not matter what play he is doing. As long as Mark knows his lines or his own personal script, his life has purpose, his part in life is meaningful—he stands self-affirmed.

Sometime after her divorce, **Jennifer Grant,** daughter of Cary Grant and Dyan Cannon, had the following amazing dream of self-affirmation or self-empowerment.

> *I am talking with friends when I suddenly realize that I have got a date that I'm supposed to make dinner for. I hurriedly go to this tiny and dark apartment. . . . I am looking for candles to light up the place, but can't find any. My date arrives looking sad. I say "Come in. I'll make you dinner." But he says "I'm not hungry." I can't figure out what to do for him, so we hug, and then he leaves. I leave this little apartment and walk into this huge home realizing this is mine. The bedroom is done. I walk past this gorgeous living room trying to figure out what I am going to do with this space. Down the hall is a beautiful sushi bar and a glass hall with nature all around, trees and water. I leave the house through a nature trail. I arrive at a theater across from my house. A friend says "Isn't it great that they're still lining up for this film." I say, "I know I've seen it, and think I'm in it."*

In that house and room symbolism usually represent the being, the person's view of their own life, a tiny and dark apartment signifies a bleak period in the dreamer's past that had the dreamer "looking for candles to light up the place." This action indicates Jennifer's optimistic spirit and her wish to alter a negative situation that at the time, could not be altered . . . thus, candles are not found. The date (probably Jennifer's ex) is offered dinner, perhaps the only nourishment that can be given him at this time, but as the date is *not* hungry he will *not* be sated. This points to some failure in mutual satisfaction where the dreamer has conscientiously tried but "cannot figure out what to do for him" or the present situation. Hugging symbolizes a nonsexual, platonic relationship and suggests that Jennifer wishes for her date's well-being and even his forgiveness. Once the date leaves, the dreamer exits the little apartment misperceived as her own, and revelation follows—her horizon is expanded.

Jennifer enters a huge home and realizes *"this* is hers"— a brighter view of life is not only hoped for but expected. Whereas the first home was tiny, the new home is "huge/ gorgeous." As the home is symbolic of the personality, this is a self-affirmative assessment. The dreamer contemplates what she will do with the space, the void in her life.

The bedroom that is already done signifies that the dreamer is emotionally ready to be romantically settled in a new relationship. Whereas the sushi bar in the home symbolizes that the dreamer is self-sustaining, the glass hall literally reflects the wish to be watched over or publicly viewed. The nature trail represents the road of self-discovery that the dreamer is eager to follow. The trail inevitably leads to a theater that is showing a film the dreamer has already seen and is in; this suggests that the dreamer has pictured what she wants in life. The fact that everyone is still lining up to view this particular film represents the wish for personal acclaim and affirms to Jennifer that she has made a correct career choice in wanting to become an actress.

Robert Goulet had a most unusual self-affirmation dream.

I was in a crowded room in some High School with crowded hallways. Everyone waiting to get to the stage. I, my wife, and some sweaty agent or promoter were all anticipating heading out for the "show" when I thought I saw a kitten scurry behind my agent's desk. I said, "Oh you have a kitten?" He, bug-eyed, turned to me and started to say, "Oh no, that's . . ." Then, what I thought was a kitten, coming around the desk behind my agent, was now a sleek, long, yellow lynx-like creature that just as swiftly stopped and jelled up into a handsome, funkily dressed African American with a charming smile. My agent was gulping and breathing heavily. My wife was frightened to death and grabbed my arm. I was giggling. I thought it was a job well done and wanted to applaud. The African American noticed that and said, "Oh, you like that, man?! Take it, it's yours."

As a high school is a place of learning, the dream involves the ability to learn something new. Similarly, the stage everyone is waiting to get to is a stage of development that is elevated, uplifted. What was seen as a kitten turns into a lynxlike creature. In other words, the kitten becomes the cat and reveals that a maturational transformation or metamorphosis has taken place. Even the agent's unfinished sentence, "Oh no, that's . . . ," symbolically suggests endless possibilities of change and growth.

Robert is delighted when the lynxlike creature swiftly jells into the "funkily dressed African American," as this is "a job well done." But the applause is for the man's ability to morph or, rather, make a smooth transition. Interestingly, the word "lynx" phonetically signifies the links that connect something together. This clarifies the dreamer's desire to form a link between generations and reveals his wish to reinvent or transform himself into whatever jells with today's societal tastes. Yet the dream is a self-affirmation of what the dreamer already knows—he has the magic within him to go with the times. As the African American passes along to Mr. Goulet the coveted secret of his wondrous transformation, he affirmatively states "take it, it's yours," which really means hold onto this, as you already own it.

The following self-affirming dream was dreamt by **Philippe Junot,** the former husband of Princess Caroline of Monaco:

> *I dreamt I was obliged to drive a Formula One in the Monaco Grand Prix. I made all effort not to look ridiculous (because of former ties, my old family relationship with Monaco). It was very hard. Cars on each side of me. Making turns with my head outside from the centrifugal force.*

This is a dream about living life in the fast lane where the road ahead is always full of turns—where high performance is expected. The cars on each side represent Philippe feeling hemmed in—his skills tested. His head is outside for some breathing space. The centrifugal force means the pressure is on.

Philippe's dream can be viewed as a metaphor for his former familial relationship with Princess Caroline and the Grimaldi family where he felt obliged to show drive and ambition. The Formula One is a lone rider with a powerful engine; it symbolizes the daring nature of the dreamer as he goes it alone—perhaps what endeared him to Monaco's grand prize, Princess Caroline. The effort was made, but "it was very hard'' is a direct reference to maintaining a marital relationship—as there were spectators everywhere. This is Philippe's self-justification, his behavioral self-affirmation.

The dream is also sexually charged; the phrase "it was very hard" refers to the physical excitement of the chase—to cross the finish line first and curry favor.

Another strong affirmation dream was dreamt during a rocky period in a love relationship. The dream belongs to the former Secretary of Commerce, **Robert Mosbacher:**

> I'm in a boat in a terrible storm, not sure I'm not going to make it but I'm sailing through it to an island I never knew existed, with a beautiful white beach, aqua water, and palm trees. I anchor the boat, having been concerned with survival and feel the peace and contentment you feel on a boat when things have gone well.

As a boat represents the structure or foundation of life, riding the boat through a storm symbolizes a stressful, rocky time when Mr. Mosbacher is being jostled about, his foundations shaken. The terrible storm reflects this difficult circumstance threatening to alter the dreamer's course of action, or, at the very least, throw him off course. But, whereas the storm should prevent moving ahead, the dreamer's perseverance drives him forward—as progression is desired. Thus, (even without muse, Georgette) the dreamer sails through rough waters to a place that he never knew existed or felt capable of reaching—an island he anchors at that represents independence and autonomy. For after all, he is no longer at sea, but alongside terra firma.

The dreamer has exceeded his own expectations. Where other men may have turned back, or worse, capsized, Robert's dream proves to him that he has gone the distance and met the challenge. What better self-affirmation than to reach the shores of contentment intact and at peace. Reaching the unknown island symbolizes the dreamer's successful quest of self-discovery—as island is the "land of I."

The following dream is an example of negative self-affirmation wherein a personal affirmation is achieved at the expense, detriment, demoralization, or minimization of another individual. This is the dream of an ex-husband of a former patient who had relayed his dream to my patient while he was still her fiancé. The day before the dream my patient had asked her fiancé to assist her in moving from her apartment. He had helped her load up shopping carts with objects from her home. This was what the ex-husband remembered of the dream and told my patient—as he claimed that this dream was what convinced him of his love for her. His dream is as follows:

You were in a shopping cart and you were blind and I was pushing you around.

The symbol of the shopping cart is two fold: It suggests a constrictive cage and at the same time objectifies the fiancée into an item pulled from a shelf. Being blind further diminishes the autonomy of the fiancée, who is viewed as being helpless, dependent, and in need of guidance and direction. She cannot see and therefore has no insight into the situation (the cramped space) she has gotten herself into.

The wheels of the cart indicate the immobility of her legs—her entrapment. The dreamer (the husband-to-be) is the one in control, the one who is doing the steering, the one who is pushing her around, which seems the dreamer's actual wish—to push his fiancée around. The dream empowers the dreamer through the demise of the fiancée's ability to fend for herself.

In reality, time would prove the dreamer (the husband) an extremely controlling and manipulative individual, one who became both verbally and physically abusive. Had my patient interpreted her fiancé's dream correctly she would never have married and would have avoided the difficult and painful experience of a divorce.

7

The Wish-Fulfillment Dream

Wish-fulfillment dreams come packaged with magic wands and should be stamped satisfaction guaranteed for they are the genies of dreams. They perform functions and are considered dreams of convenience. They fulfill desires, gratify, pacify, mend, placate, or exonerate. These dreams allow the dreamer to do what he or she cannot do in wakefulness. The actor, Christopher Reeve, who is paralyzed from the neck down, has told Joan Jedell, publisher and editor of *The Hampton Sheet,* "In my dreams I go everywhere, I go on wonderful trips with my wife and children." Wish-fulfillment dreams may also include consolation dream motifs of visitations by deceased loved ones (see dream of Victoria Principal). Freud, however, makes the claim that most anxiety dreams are really wish fulfillments that have been disguised and repressed. The following are several wish-fulfillment dreams. The first was dreamt by the soprano **Deborah Voigt**:

> *I'm on stage acting, singing my part, Aida, but the end of the opera changes. Instead of dying with my lover in the tomb, I reach out and punch my father. I grab my lover's hand and run off. Every one goes along with this happy ending. I get a standing ovation.*

At first this seems a work-related dream designed to shatter the monotony of playing the same tragic role of Aida, but the implications are far-reaching. Shakespeare's notion that we are all player's on the stage of life following our intended scripts irks Deborah enough to make a bold and liberating, unexpected move on stage whereby she gains control over the story, the action, and her life by changing the end of the opera. Thus, the dream invokes the defiant wish to break the restrictions and prescribed ways of thinking that ultimately control the outcomes of our affairs, as Deborah takes destiny in her own hands.

The dream contains the infantile wish to dominate the father, as a critical attitude emerges that questions his ethics and belief systems. The daughter is empowered with the freedom of choice as Deborah's Aida is a child freed from the oppression of parental expectations. She is no longer compliant. The father is punched but not before Deborah has reached out in what appears a failed communication. The lovers run off from the tomb, a womb substitute, breaking ties with symbols of containment, in a departure that represents the death of an old life. Deborah is reborn and on the verge of a creative evolution, but she is not there yet, which is why she needs the self-affirming standing ovation at the end of the dream. This represents the need for societal approval: she still wants to be sure the crowd is with her. This suggests that Deborah's self-esteem is greater than her sense of self-love.

The following wish-fulfillment dream, dreamt by **Vivica A. Fox,** the beautiful heroine of the movie *Independence Day*, combines with a self-affirming element:

I am sitting in my seat at the Oscars. I am wearing a pink dress. Suddenly I hear them call my name. I have won an Oscar. I get up and walk down the aisle and everyone is applauding.

This typical wish-fulfillment dream was dreamt two weeks before the night of the Oscars and reveals what any young actress desires: to win the critical acclaim of her peers. "Sitting in my seat," a symbolic representation of being one among many, is contrasted with getting up from the seat, which is the wish to rise above the anonymity. Hearing them "call my name," is the wish for recognition, as is the applauding, which serves as a validation of Vivica's talent. The applause is what makes this dream one of self-affirmation, as applause always represents approval.

"Walking down the aisle" makes one think of taking a vow and gives spiritual meaning and poignancy to the desire for success, as the image brings to mind weddings, churches, temples of worship, and the dedication of purpose . . . in other words, commitment. The word "aisle" also has the phonetic rendering of the word "I'll," which is a very affirmative *I will*.

Everyone applauding not only represents the wish for societal approval but also represents Vivica applauding herself and her accomplishments. Thus, Vivica thinks highly of herself, and why not, as her dress signifies that she is in the pink. Similarly, "sitting in *my* seat" is a confirmation of belonging to this exclusive Hollywood group. It is important to note that the dreamer never physically takes hold of the golden statue, which suggests that the material prize is worth less than the emotional reward of being honored by her talented contemporaries.

Peter Lawson-Johnston, the head of the Guggenheim Foundation, has had a most interesting wish-fulfillment dream. The dream is as follows:

The Guggenheim Museum has had a branch in Venice for some time, but I dreamt that there would be lots of Guggenheims sprouting up in the future. I was traveling abroad with my wife and instead of seeing McDonald's along the road, we'd see Guggenheims.

The image of "Guggenheims along the road" instead of McDonald's suggests that the dreamer is fusing high culture with popular culture in a way that allows culture to disseminate throughout the country. In other words, the dreamer wishes to make art accessible to the masses—and desires that art be consumed within the social milieu on a day to day basis. Similarly, as McDonald's boasts "over a billion served" the dream contains the noble intention of serving humanity—feeding the visual senses by serving up the grandeur of art.

As the viewing of art is connected with nourishment and fulfillment, museums are symbolically exchanged with food chains—going to a museum should be as common an event as eating. Art is imagined as food for thought. As a McDonald's architectural facade suggests that a heavenly taste experience awaits one beyond its famed golden arches, the Guggenheim, with its lofty inclined circles, suggests that the art experience should elevate the spirit of mankind—stimulate its taste for the aesthetic. The wish of the dream is to make art as available as fast food, and it is thus a measure of what has been the humanitarian spirit noted among the Guggenheims.

The following is an example of a negative wish-fulfill-ment dream wherein the wish manifests itself in the form of a frightening nightmare:

Just after I had gotten married I dreamt that I was sleeping in my bedroom. Suddenly I noticed that a life-sized stone statue of a saint was standing in front of my bed. It was a female saint whose face resembled that of my mother's, although her expression was stern and somber. Just as I was wondering what this statue was doing in my room, the stone statue opened its eyes and stared at me. I screamed and awoke.

The dream symbolizes the maternal separation anxiety of the dreamer, who had just gotten married. The marrying event is the antecedent of the dream visualization—being gazed upon by a stone statue that resembles the dreamer's mother. The dreamer's wish is to remain watched over and protected by her mother.

In a further wish, the watching—done in stony silence—signifies that there will be no judgment call or criticism imparted from the stone entity, or mother. But, the stone statue—symbolic of something inanimate or dead—also represents the guilt of the dreamer who, by the act of growing up, marrying, and leaving her mother's house, imagines that she has killed off the need for maternal protection. Thus, the face of the statue is stern and somber.

Therefore, although the fulfilled wish of being watched over is a consolation of sorts, it is negatively received—the dreamer screams because even in the deepest recesses of her unconscious she is aware of the dangers of her own dependency and lack of autonomy.

8

The Oedipal or Libidinous Dream

The classic Freudian oedipal dream is concerned mainly with the satisfying and gratifying of sexual urges and fantasies, particularly in respect to the primary love object—mother. These dreams are aggressive in nature and are often fraught with violent symbolism where instinctual forces are at work and the animal passions are uninhibited. They often reveal the fear of castration. Within this category are masturbatory fantasies.

The following oedipal/libidinous dream is **G. Gordon Liddy**'s, radio host, former FBI agent, former special assistant to the Secretary of the Treasury for Organized Crime, former member of the Justice Department, and former Senior Security Advisor for the Committee to Reelect President Nixon:

> *I discover myself to be in a very large house with multiple multiple rooms. I am in the company of a young woman for whose safety and well-being I have somehow become responsible. It's never made clear how or why. There is a romantic and/or sexual relationship there. There are bad or antagonistic people outside the house and they are a threat. As I go through the house I am trying to figure out how I am going to protect this*

female and accomplish some mission which involves leaving the house and going somewhere else. The house turns out to be floating on a body of water; sometimes it is a mere river and sometimes it is a very large body of water but there's always land in the prospect and I am trying to get to the land with the female. When I get to land, the hostile forces are hot in pursuit and there's an edifice like a lighthouse. I have somehow become armed with a firearm. . . . I get to the top of the stairs of the lighthouse . . . have this female there, and people come up the stairs, and there's a gun battle and I kill people left and right.

This is an oedipal dream where the image of the father has been extended onto anonymous others making him seem many people instead of one person and, therefore, nondescript. The very large house is the mother, as is the young woman "for whose safety and well-being" the dreamer is somehow responsible. By reversal, the dreamer transfers the protecting role that the mother plays onto himself, which is why he is "never clear how or why" he is now the protector. The romantic and/or sexual relationship is the oedipal fantasy/desire for the mother. The bad, antagonistic people outside the house represent the dreamer's father whose extended image looms large. The threat is fear of castration. The dreamer figures out how to protect the female from hostile forces (the father) and accomplish his mission (oedipal fulfillment), which "involves leaving the house," to escape the wrath of the father.

The house afloat is a birth vision in that the dreamer is in a large body of water where "land is always in the prospect." Hostile forces are in "hot pursuit," but reaching the lighthouse (the wish for empowerment), becoming armed with a firearm (phallic symbol of manliness and strength), and "getting to the top of the stairs" (sexual activity) assures the dreamer that he may look down on his aggressors, as he feels bigger and taller. He bonds with the lighthouse as edifice and phallus. The gun battle wherein the dreamer kills people "right and left" is really the infantile oedipal wish to do away with the father. The gunfire presumably means that bullets are flying, which symbolizes sexual activity—the culmination of the orgasm. The wish for sexual climax is gratified.

But there is another interpretation of Liddy's dream. The house with "multiple multiple" rooms may symbolize the United States of America, or even the White House. Guarding this home would reveal the ethical, moral standpoint of the dreamer to protect and defend his country from outside, foreign, hostile forces. The dreamer's dangerous mission to reach the lighthouse, which symbolizes self-illumination and truth, suggests that Liddy is looking for answers. The danger involved in the mission reveals the dreamer's heroic nature, for only through personal sacrifice can "the safety and well-being" of the country (America) be preserved. This indicates the patriotic spirit prominent within the dream and the dreamer.

9

The Problem-Solving Dream

P roblem-solving dreams are like Grimm's fairy tale *The Shoemaker's Elves* because they industriously look for answers, solutions, and decisions. They reveal how our unconscious mind continues to process information and seek throughout the night the completion or closure of conscious issues. These dreams are also a measure of the creative aspect of the unconscious and reveal what can be accomplished without the distractions of daily living. Many inventions have been dreamt or formalized during the night. Elias Howe claims to have discovered how to make a workable needle for his sewing machine after it miraculously appeared in his dream. (See discovery dreams motif.) Coleridge claims to have dreamt all fifty-five lines of his poem *Kubla Khan*. Many memorable scenes from Ingmar Bergman's films *Wild Strawberries* and *Smiles of a Summer Night* are exact copies of his own dreams. In the scene from the film the *Seventh Seal* where death holds hands with the dying and leads them up a mountainside, one is aware of the nocturnal dream quality of the content. Supposedly many conquerors, such as Alexander the Great and Julius Caesar, have been guided by their dreams, as they believed in their prophetic essence. Even Napoléon kept a dream journal wherein he jotted down the details of his dreams, which often envisioned military strategies. These strategies were often inspirational in the planning of his campaigns. Similarly, numerous musicians such as Mozart and Schumann claim to have composed melodies while unconscious. Richard Wagner wrote about musical ideas that came to him during what he called a trancelike state (a hypnagogic state somewhere between waking and sleeping). It is most probable that Winston Churchill imagined while in this same state that his father Lord Randolph appeared to him in his art studio to question him on the twentieth century.

The following are examples of problem-solving dreams: This first dream was dreamt by the world's greatest tenor, **Luciano Pavarotti:**

I was at the movies watching Orson Wells [sic]playing Othello. I was in the audience when suddenly I took Orson Wells' place. I was watching myself playing the role of Orson Wells, a hero of mine, thinking this is very presumptuous of me because Orson Wells is such a great actor.

The time of this dream has particular relevance as it was dreamt during Luciano Pavarotti's first *Othello* performance, a role he did not usually play or think right for himself. The great performer who is used to being watched becomes the watcher in the audience in an attempt to relieve the pressure from being on stage—to try to replicate the part of Othello as grandly enacted on the screen by Orson Welles, Luciano's hero. Thus, the dream seeks to resolve an actual problem.

By dreaming of replacing Orson Wells as Othello, Pavarotti reinforces his confidence—enables himself to do what he feels incapable of doing. But before Pavarotti gains strength from his hero's performance, he masters it by assimilation. Drawing from Orson's "well" is symbolically and artistically nourishing and sustaining. Bonding with the inner strength his hero represents enables Pavarotti to clarify and develop within himself the way to play the part. In general, a hero symbol arises when the ego needs strengthening or when the mind needs assistance in some task it feels it cannot accomplish unaided by external help. Pavarotti's move from seat to screen is his liberating wish to break from any fixed or confining pattern of existence—symbolically, the dreamer achieves transcendence. On the big screen he can assume a *larger than life* image. Feeling "presumptuous" by watching himself play Orson's role expresses the humility of a great artist who is trying to achieve the full potential of his individual self.

The following problem-solving dream was dreamt by **Monique van Vooren:** actress, author, singer, and closest friend of Rudolf Nureyev:

> I went to a house that was dilapidated. It was scary. To enter the house there were many crickety stairs. But when I entered the door the hallway was luxurious, beautiful—the lighting was low. But on the floor there were the lines of chalk police draw to indicate a body was there—and a harsh light was on that spot. Someone had been killed, and I ran upstairs to a room, and Rudolf Nureyev was in this room. He was in a crib tied up.

The above dream reflects the deep concern that the dreamer had for her closest friend, Rudolf Nureyev, and imaginatively comes up with a solution to save him from harm's way. Concern for his well-being is shown by the dreamer visualizing him "tied up in a crib" where "crib" represents a *safety* zone. Similarly, the "crib" symbolizes the dreamer's wish to protect Nureyev in motherly fashion from a perceived danger, in that the "chalk lines" at the bottom of the stairs indicate that death is close by. The "harsh light" highlighting those ominous lines of chalk is the stark, *harsh reality* of her friend's private lifestyle . . . being promiscuous in an era of violence and AIDS.

In that "houses" in dreams represent the body, a "dilapidated," run-down exterior can represent the wearing away of one's physical being through disease. And although somewhat afraid, the dreamer bravely enters the door finding the interior *(the mind, the soul of her friend)* still "luxurious and beautiful." Although "climbing up the stairs" is the wish for sexual relationship, within the dream Nureyev can be possessed and/or loved only platonically. The mother, as one who births and *cribs,* is the rescuer, which allows this dream to be viewed as a rescue fantasy wherein the dreamer has to overcome certain fears or hardships. As a "house" can also symbolize the *mind,* stepping inside the house symbolizes that the dreamer is looking beyond the surface and making an effort to understand the life inside of the home, the mind and/or the *lifestyle* of her friend. And although there is seductiveness *("the lighting was low"),* danger is harboring nearby for someone has been killed.

The image of Nureyev being "tied-up" could symbolize time and mean that a delay is hoped for. This symbol may also represent the dreamer's wish that things be under her control or dominance—that Nureyev be *submissive* to her demands. Because, in reality, the dreamer is aware that she cannot stop her friend from that which will inevitably kill him and/or bring about his demise.

The following problem-solving dream was dreamt by the designer, **Emanuel Ungaro,** who visualized within his dream the entire theme of his next fashion show:

> *In my dream I am starting my next fashion show with the sound of voices as well as the music from the film* Casablanca. *Then I hear the voices of Humphrey Bogart and Ingrid Bergman intertwining with the famous "Play It Again, Sam"* . . . *All of that in the dark, just before the first girl (model) steps onto the runway.*

An inspirational tone is created within the dream as voices are heard—music is played. Ungaro visualizes the theme he will use for his upcoming fashion show—the timeless romantic drama tinged with a bit of danger and intrigue. The dream reveals Ungaro's wish to create a classic collection filled with the kind of visual drama and excitement that will make his fashion designs as memorable as the movie classic *Casablanca.* The phrase "Play it again, Sam," symbolizes Ungaro's desire to do another show, another collection, the desire to repeat past successes. The phrase also serves as introduction to the song "As Time Goes By," where "fundamental rules still apply"—create something classically beautiful, timeless! Thus, the dream reveals Ungaro's preoccupation with his life work—the task of creating a dramatic statement through fashion—and reflects Ungaro's nostalgia for his prior collections. The phrase "all of this in the dark" symbolizes that Ungaro creates *internally* from an imaginative spirit, an inner muse.

The most memorable scene of *Casablanca* takes place on

an airport runway where Ingrid Bergman gives her final good-bye to Humphrey Bogart. Amazingly, this scene is symbolically linked to another runway—the fashion show runway or catwalk. This reveals to what extent Ungaro intertwines his world of fashion with the romantic fantasy world of movies.

The following problem-solving dream was dreamt by **Warren Avis,** founder of Avis Rent A Car, and CEO of Avis Enterprises:

> *I had just come from the bomb base. I had to get somewhere. There was no transportation. I dreamt there was a terrible need for ground transportation. That's how I started Avis.*

When he was not flying as an air force combat officer, Mr. Avis could not get anywhere on land, as transportation was scarce. His dream, therefore, was based on solving a real problem. But in order to come up with solutions one must first be aware of what needs to be solved. Thus, there is the recognition, "I had to get somewhere." This symbolizes the desire to get ahead in the world, to go forward, to progress, and it also suggests drive. "I had to . . ." intensifies a sense of urgency and a spirit of determination. Noticing an existing external need reflects a perceptive and empathic nature—the ability to look beyond oneself. Mr. Avis, having just come down from the clouds, is on solid ground, involved with realistic goals.

The "need for ground transportation" suggests there is much to be covered and not enough time—but the *"wheels"* of inspiration have already been set in motion. As ground transportation moves one from one place to another, there is also the wish for social interaction—to move about in society. Thus, the wish of the dream may be to connect people, to bring people closer to their aspirations.

The following problem-solving dream was dreamt by the very brilliant **Esther Dyson,** who heads the yearly PC Forum:

> *I was with some people in a multi-story building which had no stairs below the second floor. We wanted to get out, and I said, "No problem; we can use the elevator." We got to the elevator and it had no buttons for the floors, just an empty hole. "No problem," I said, "we can use text search." I typed in "first floor" and then woke up.*

As buildings symbolize the self by housing the individual, Esther Dyson's multi-story structure defines her complex, multifaceted personality. The building's foundation, having "no stairs below the second floor," is not structurally rooted. By hovering two stories above the ground, the dreamer is made inaccessible and unreachable by ordinary means—in computer jargon this translates to access denied. For Dyson is on a higher level: at the very least two flights above everyone else in the cerebral realm of reason and intellect. Thus, the dream involves getting down to earth, but the descent is problematic.

Esther's descent represents the quest for self-knowledge. She delves beneath the surface into the "empty hole," the uncharted places of the unconscious, which is why the elevator has no numbered "floor buttons" to push or to locate one's position. But although Dyson is searching for emotional redemption—a deeper level of herself—her method of descent relies on the wondrous technological function of a computer's "text search." Thus, even the dreamer's departure from the cerebral to the instinctual realm necessitates high-tech know-how rather than feeling—indicating that in Dyson's dream world technology is the liberating factor!

10

The Examination Dream

xamination dreams can be viewed as stimulants that are meant to keep us on our toes. They represent our self-critical, conscientious, and dutiful natures. They stem from early memories of failed attempts or enterprises, which serve as negative models of what not to do. These dreams seek to maintain structure and discipline wherein we may be punishing or chastising ourselves as a way of keeping ourselves in check. They emphasize the importance of preparation and condemn procrastination and unawareness. They are the dreams of the mythical Atlas who was fated to carry the burden of the world on his shoulders. Examination dreams are dreamt by successful and ambitious individuals and they usually occur before a responsible activity. Yet, these dreams are also regarded as an indignant protest, in that an explanation, which serves as a consolation and reminder of our past successes or abilities to perform, is often put forward in our defense. Thus, the dream is a mixed brew of self-criticism and self-consolation, where reproach often turns into a congratulatory pat on the back.

The following are examples of examination dreams: the first was dreamt by **Arie L. Kopelman,** president of Chanel, Inc.

About once a year (for many years) I dream about a huge amount of reading still to be done for a college course. I'm back in my senior year and must pass this course to graduate . . . but for some reason, I've let all the reading slide until a week before the final exam. The word "panic" takes on new meaning! The pressure mounts to a point where it seems that absolutely no problem could possibly be more monumental . . . when I wake up, there is enormous relief in knowing that it was only a dream. After that, virtually any problem I face in business seems small in comparison.

This recurring examination dream is dreamt by the most industrious people because the repeated self-reproach serves as a way of keeping them in check. Perfectionists panic precisely because they feel there is always more to be done. Thus, the dream itself is an assignment in preparedness—the dreamer is the instructor shaking his finger against procrastination. Fearing one will not pass or measure up to self-expectations underscores a conscientious nature and reflects Arie's concerns about meeting society's deadlines. "Panic" is redefined in a way that makes it more tolerable, as Arie makes the realization that any business problem he encounters will be small in comparison to the demands of academia.

But the college course is the course of life, and the wish of the dream is to let slide the rigid time frames of the work-a-day world of business, where to pass or graduate means to transcend to a higher plateau. Arie is on a quest of self-discovery, as a "huge amount of reading still to be done" symbolizes that there are many pages left unturned within the dreamer.

The following examination dream was dreamt by former governor **Mario Cuomo:**

> *I show up in school only to be told that there is an exam about to take place that I did not know about or prepare for.*

Mr. Cuomo's dream has deliberately thrown him a loop: he was neither given the date nor time of an exam "about to take place." But, by creating an unexpected event, he can effectively test himself in uncharted waters as a means of self-assessment. In other words, the dream *itself* is a test—a crisis situation the dreamer must deal with. An examination dream where the dreamer shows up unprepared shows the urgency of self-confrontation and symbolizes that the dreamer may have remembered having made an oversight in the past and is modestly chastising himself. This is a judgmental dream where the dreamer is humbled and placed somewhere between pride, consolation, and critical evaluation. Ironically, this type of dream is usually dreamt by exceptional students who feel proud of their accomplishments. The self-reproaches come from a fear of not being able to maintain a certain level of attainment—a self-imposed standard of greatness. The consolation is in the form of an indignant protest, as the dreamer objects to not having known about the exam.

These examination dreams are anguished over precisely because the dreamers are most demanding on themselves. These dreamers are scrupulously perceptive. These dreams underscore a conscientious and diligent nature—concerns are on meeting the demands of society. Control is an issue; value is placed on knowledge and preparation. The wish of the dream is to adapt to the vicissitudes of the outside world, to overcome the unpredictability of life, its surprises and inconsistencies.

11

The Initiation Dream

Initiation dreams are usually connected to significant, transitional, or critical phases in our lives, such as in early childhood, puberty, the onset of middle age, and before death, when we are contemplating making a break from a current life style or life situation that is felt to be rigid, restrictive, or final, superficial, immature, or meaningless. The initiation dream is the Che Guevara of dreams looking to liberate the country of our selves. The dream asks for release from or transcendence over any confining or claustrophobic pattern of existence for it desires to move toward a more superior or mature stage of development.

The aim of the dream is to tame the wild, errant, juvenile, or primitive nature, and thus it has a civilizing or spiritual purpose. The dream is on a quest of self-discovery of the human psyche whose essence escapes us. It seeks revelation, harmony, and balance. It looks for individuation while trying to feel a totality and wholeness, an affinity and kinship with the world. These dreams often include themes of death and resurrection or restitution wherein mythological creatures such as witches, wild beasts, devils, and snakes often present ordeals or trials of strength that we must triumph over. In essence, these dreams are heroic attempts that try to integrate consciousness with unconsciousness to illuminate and expand the wider personality.

The following initiation dream of my dear deceased friend **Ludovic Autet** is of particular significance because it was dreamt a year before he died. The dream itself reveals his strong intuitive wisdom, as the dream foreshadows his ultimate initiation into the hereafter.

> *I dreamt I was in my bedroom when suddenly from a long hall I saw two dogs coming toward my room, one yellow, the other black. I shut my door, but somehow the dark dog came through the door and got into my bedroom. It looked menacing, like a panther, but when it climbed onto my bed I embraced it, and we lay embracing, sleeping.*

In Ludovic's mystical dream the unconscious advances in the shape of a black dog that thrusts itself upon the scene—going through a closed door. This symbolizes the powerful, intellectual, and moral effort needed to examine this dark, closed off, evening side of our psyche. The door—as an entrance into the unknown—is always frightening. But, in heroic style, Ludovic confronts the aggressor on his own—the yellow dog that represents fear is kept outside. Embracing the dangerous panther reveals Ludovic's fearless love of challenge.

Like Sir Galahad after the Grail, Ludovic succeeds; he gets in touch with his instincts and soothes the savage beast. That he disarms and tames the menacing panther reveals his natural charm and seductiveness. This initiation dream signifies that Ludovic is on the verge of enlightenment, for in order to reach the light, one must first go through the darkness of the tunnel!

The following initiation dream was dreamt by the director, **Milos Forman:**

> *I am standing in front of our little house in a small town called Caslav, with my hand on the door knob. I hear the sweet voices of my mother, father and brothers talking inside. The house is surrounded by a garden, where, not ten yards away from me, partly hidden in the bushes, a witch is hiding: a scraggy old creature with wild graying hair, long fingernails, toothless mouth, dressed in dirty rags. Her hand signals me to step away from the door. I won't do that. I laugh at her, provoke her: come and get me. I feel safe with my hand on the door. Then, faster than I can open the door and enter the safety of the house, the witch grabs me and throws me into never ending space. I am falling and falling, passing indescribable surfaces which keep changing from smooth to rough. When the space is smooth I feel elated and happy. When the space is crumpled I cringe, suffer fear and feel utterly miserable.*

Pleasurable feelings are transformed into painful anxieties in this recurrent childhood dream that contains a taboo fantasy common among small boys, wherein self-punishment is inflicted as a means of lessening guilt. What is "partly hidden in the bushes" are the submerged sexual urges making themselves known. The door "knob" is a phallic symbol that empowers the small boy to feel brave enough to provoke the witch. But, the boy is literally caught with his hand on the door (a symbol of a forbidden act) and is punished accordingly by the witch, who grabs him and sends him falling into "never ending space." Whereas dreams of falling represent a surrender to an erotic temptation, the motion of falling unsupported also reveals the self-reliant, independent spirit of the dreamer.

Surfaces relate to the sense of touch and the feelings that arise from it. The smooth, extended falling space represents sexual activity with its indescribable, pleasurable sensation, whereas the crumpled space refers to the sexual culmination—something that has collapsed. This is why there is no longer elation but only a cringing—a drawing back that makes the dreamer "feel utterly miserable."

Dreams of falling or descending are considered a type of initiation wherein the dreamer is seeking a deeper self-knowledge. Similarly, dreams dealing with varying sensations, such as surfaces ranging from smooth to rough, may suggest the evolving process of maturation. The witch is the negative anima (the feminine part of male consciousness) that makes the dreamer develop an intuitive sense by literally unearthing his unconscious personality in the "never ending space" he falls through, the profound inner depths of introspection.

Another interesting initiation dream was dreamt by the actress, **Traci Lind:**

I am in a big wooden home like a barn, in a long hall-way with many doors leading onto other rooms. I come out and see a tree on a low hill. As I walk to the tree there is the outline of a black leopard standing on his hind legs. It is very beautiful. Behind him, low on the horizon, there are twelve full moons rising over this low stone wall. The leopard, with his back to the

*moons, is talking to me, lecturing me in a man's voice.
I am resigned and angry at the same time, feeling love
and fear, resigned to the fate of it. He is explaining that
he has to kill me now. There is no way around it.*

An initiation dream such as Traci's is usually connected
to a period of transition in life, as it reflects the need for liberation from any confining or restrictive state of being. The
black leopard is Traci's self and represents her passions, her
instinctual side. But the black leopard is visualized without
spots because it has lost its light, the golden part of its essence; this suggests that Traci is in need of illumination.
Thus, the leopard is the accuser, the lecturer *(the animus, the
inner masculine part of female consciousness)*, the powerful
one that has to kill off the part of Traci that needs to be subdued or brought to submission in order that a superior stage
of development will begin. This transcendence may only be
reached through the death of her old self which is why Traci
is resigned to this fate. But this is a resignation or surrender
in a spiritual sense—an acceptance of a higher ideal.

Being up against a stone wall means Traci is at an impasse, but the wall is low enough to see what is shining beyond; The "twelve full moons rising" suggest that
ascendancy awaits Traci on the other side. This is the wish to
ascend to an elevated point of view so as to gain an increased
awareness. Because the moon is associated with love, ro-
mance, and the feminine nature, twelve moons underscore
the dominating power of the feminine. Facing the moons
means Traci wishes to confront her femininity and find enlightenment in an otherwise bleak and blackened scenario.

The following initiation dream was dreamt by the impre-
sario **Don King:**

I was pondering the future when I heard a rumbling in my head. My hair was uncurling and going straight up, rising. Pim. Pim. Pim. Each hair shot up toward the heavens. I felt I was being pulled up by God.

This is an initiation dream connected to a period of transition in the dreamer's life, and it alludes to the need for liberation from a restricted state of being. The dreamer is aroused by a rumbling sound in his head, much like a Dionysian thunder rite celebrating the wildness of a free spirit. Don's hair uncurling symbolizes the wish for transcendence or release from any constraining lifestyle, and it reflects an ideological change in progress. Similarly, hair extending represents the full growth potential of the individual. As each hair shoots up toward the heavens, the dreamer is wired in to the universe, connected to higher levels of consciousness, striving for attainment and ascendancy. This is the wish to rise up in the world and a statement of self-assurance.

Although hair standing on end usually represents fear, the dream, in a bold reversal of stereotypic imagery, transforms fear into grandiose feelings of empowerment and great strength. Therefore, the dream undermines stereotypic thinking by not conforming to standard views. Moreover, the hair ''going straight up'' does so against the laws of gravity or against the odds; this reinforces Mr. King's individualism. ''Being pulled up'' by God represents the wish for illumination and the wish for recognition. Mr. King claims that his hair looks the way it does today because the dream actually produced a change in his physical appearance. What is more significant is that his hair combed upward is a symbol of the optimistic spirit he felt in his dream.

Another interesting initiation dream was dreamt by the actress **Sarah Buxton:**

> *In the jungle someone is chasing me. I'm trying to get to the native music in the distance. The chaser is getting closer. It's hard to run, the ground is wet, I'm barefoot. I see this hill, there's fire and loud tribal music, a celebration. I can't get where I want to go. The chaser disappears, and I'm having a dance-fight with a cobra. I want to get up the hill. After this dance-fight I'm flying, gliding over the ocean.*

Not knowing who or what is chasing Sarah through the jungle symbolizes a problem Sarah does not want to face, or a problem that she has overlooked. Thus, the problem pursues the dreamer in the form of an unseen chaser, bringing difficulties Sarah must overcome "to get where she wants to go." It is hard to run because the ground is wet and Sarah is barefoot—which in the singular sense of the word signifies that Sarah's sole or (soul) is exposed. This represents the dreamer's wish to be in touch with the fertile, wet earth. The more vague the pursuer, the more unaware the dreamer is of her instinctual desires, and the more imperative the need for intuition and self-realization.

In the jungle, the dense forest of the unconscious, an initiation rite begins with native music and fire, representing the force of passions. Sarah must rid herself of her inner demons in order to come to terms with her individual spirit and celebrate herself. There is the ordeal of getting up the hill, the trial of strength as symbolized by the "dance-fight" with a cobra. But the cobra symbolizes Sarah's instinctual side and therefore transcendence, as the one who is chased becomes the chaser in a confrontation that Sarah wins. The "dance-fight" suggests that Sarah bonds with the cobra through sexual union and with her true nature, her animal instincts. Sarah takes the animal inside herself and makes it her companion, her guardian spirit. Thus, at the end of the dream Sarah is elevated above and beyond the hill, as she is able to fly and glide over the ocean. This is the wished for experience of rebirth and spiritual release that accompanies a gained sense of independence and inner harmony.

The following initiation dream was dreamt by **Chris Royer,** supermodel:

> *I am walking down a crescent-shaped, white, sandy beach. Suddenly, a man appears from nowhere. With the sun in my eyes, I see him only as a silhouette. As he comes near, a white sphere falls from the blue sky into his outstretched hand. He passes the sphere to me.*

The dream begins near water, which represents a new beginning, and it has luminous content: the sun in the dreamer's eyes. As one cannot look directly into the face of God, the man who suddenly appears from nowhere is only seen in silhouette. He performs magic as a white sphere falls from the sky into his outstretched hand. The white sphere is a representation of the world the dreamer wants to hold in her hand, and is a measure of the control gained when it is given to her. This marks a transition, or the symbolic passing of power—possibly from father to daughter—as the sun often symbolizes the father.

The man is a silhouette and as such only gives a part of the picture, offering the outline without revealing the sense of what is inside. But the more unaware the dreamer is of what she sees, the greater the need for intuition and trust. This is an initiation dream of sorts as the sphere is the start point around which everything spins, and a concept of self-awareness. Thus, the dreamer has sensed a higher level of understanding, an enlightenment, but has also accepted or come to terms with a spiritual or emotional responsibility now that the sphere, or ball, is in her hands. The dream also indicates the dreamer's wish to be open, to be able to receive.

12

The Prophetic Dream

The prophetic dream, the questioner of all dreams, is the most introspective of all, as it looks mostly for meaning and answers; it anticipates the future, calculates and fathoms in the fashion of Nostradamus. Since ancient times the Bible cites numerous examples of prophetic dreams that come to pass. These dreams fit into the realm of the uncanny and can be defined as possessing foresight and perception. They can be thought of as premonitions, which may, however, be nothing more than unrealized and unremembered déjà vu experiences that are the antecedents of the dreamed event that comes to pass. These are intuitive dreams whose veridical nature cannot be scientifically determined or measured with our present knowledge. The following are some examples of prophetic dreams.

The first prophetic dream was dreamt by **Pierre Salinger:**

In August, 1982, I was on vacation in Corsica for one month when I dreamt I heard in my brain the words "you should be aware that one of the worst terrorist attacks will take place in Paris in the last week." I left for Paris immediately, and the day after I arrived a bomb exploded in a Jewish restaurant/bakery.

Having just been working with ABC, covering terrorism, Mr. Salinger's dream may be viewed as a measure of his conscientiousness, for his dream is deeply committed and connected to his work of the moment. Even on vacation, it is not permissible to let down one's guard. Thus, Mr. Salinger's dream commands that he should be aware of the evils of society—the dream gives the warning to be wary. But, interestingly, in that Mr. Salinger is half French, the dream may reflect a recognition of some personal turmoil or upheaval wherein the city of Paris symbolizes the dreamer himself. In other words, if a difficult situation is not dealt with, it will become explosive.

The prophetic nature of the dream cannot be discounted, as the dream's prediction actually occurred in 1982—a Jewish restaurant/bakery was blown up in Paris. The dream may be viewed, therefore, as a measure of Mr. Salinger's sensitive and intuitive nature. One wonders, though, if the prophecy was referring to something that has not yet happened—something far more catastrophic than the 1982 terrorist attack—for the phrase "In the last week" is worded in biblical fashion and brings biblical significance to the dream. In Hebraic biblical interpretation a week means seven years—the last week, therefore, may allude to the end of all days or Armageddon; the "worst terrorist" may be euphemistic for the ultimate biblical demon, Satan.

(It must be noted that Mr. Salinger first told me this dream on August 30, 1997, hours before the unspeakable tragedy occurred "in Paris, in the last week"—the fatal car crash of Diana, Princess of Wales, and her companion, Dodi Fayed. Indeed, had not the frenzied pack of paparazzi in hot pursuit "terrorized" the car that desperately tried to speed away? Adding to the strangeness of Pierre telling me his dream just prior to another tragic event is that the very next dream I interpreted—four hours later—was Soheir Khashoggi's. Soheir is the sister of Adnan Khashoggi, and the aunt of Dodi Fayed. An eerie coincidence!)

The following prophetic dream was dreamt by the designer, **Oleg Cassini:**

> *I have arrived by boat. Many people greet me with "I'm so glad you could come." I'm in Hollywood surrounded by movie stars, recognizing faces from American movies, like Clark Gable. A beautiful dark-haired actress with light eyes and golden skin is in love with me. I'm a famous fashion designer.*

Christmas 1936, Oleg Cassini was living in fascist Italy, with war imminent; the way of life was disintegrating. Oleg's dream is a wish fulfillment but also a prophetic tool, in that the future has proved it true in every way. Indeed, Mr. Cassini came to the United States, married the consummate beautiful movie star (Gene Tierney), and became a fashion designer, perhaps *the* most famous and respected designer of the century; his name has become a household word.

However, what seems a prophetic dream is really Oleg coming to grips with an awareness of his own talents and his desire to fulfill them. The dream bolsters his self-confidence. In other words, the dreamer's self knowledge inspires him with the drive needed to fulfill his wish consciously. By surrounding himself with another world, another setting, he has recognized all that he wants in life.

"Arriving by boat," reflects a wish to cross over to another world. The boat symbolizes the rite of passage. Being welcomed from the water represents birth—a new life, a new start. People saying ''I'm so glad you could come reflects the desire to be well received and appreciated. Importantly, Oleg's arrival has been noted—''to have arrived'' means having become successful. But the wish is not just granted; it must be earned. By envisioning himself a fashion designer Oleg will live his dream, as a designer symbolizes someone with a scheme, plan, or purpose.

The following telepathic dream was dreamt in the morning of June 6, 1968—at 4:43 A.M.—moments before Robert F. Kennedy was pronounced dead, at 1:44 A.M. Pacific time—during the exact time of the assassination. The dream was dreamt by the author, **John Davis,** first cousin of Jacqueline Bouvier Kennedy Onassis:

> *I was being engulfed in an ocean of excrement or human sewage. It was falling down from the sky like rain and I was drowning in it. I knew something horrible, something catastrophic had happened but I was unsure of what it was.*

Mr. Davis had been up late working on a chapter from his book *The Bouviers: From Waterloo to the Kennedys and Beyond.* Ironically, the chapter discussed Bobby Kennedy's candidacy for the presidency, and envisioned the possible restoration of John F. Kennedy's spirit in the White House. Considering the task at hand and the familial relationship of Mr. Davis to President Kennedy, there may be a fair amount of the empathic in the telepathic. For John Davis seems to have picked up his premonitory thoughts simultaneously with the occurrence of the event. In other words, the dream does not come to pass—*the dream is during the passing*!

It must be noted that John Davis had been filled with grim

apprehension upon the announcement of R.F.K's candidacy. But in that he awoke from his gruesome presentiment one minute before R.F.K. was declared dead, it is entirely reasonable to view this dream as more than just a condemnation of corrupt and corrosive society, as it appears one of deep telepathic nature.

In Revelation 8:10 the Bible refers to "a great star [that] fell from heaven, burning like a torch, on a third of the rivers . . ." as being a symbol of foreboding destruction. Similarly, when a dream reveals something ominous coming from above "falling down from the sky," it is usually viewed as a warning signal. Whereas "rain" is a birth symbol of nourishment, survival, and purification, the raining of "excrement" or "human sewage" is its horrific opposite—a death symbol of decay and putrefaction.

The "ocean" which symbolizes a birth vision, becomes an "ocean of excrement" and represents a deathly vision. "Excrement" is a symbolic image that evokes being defiled. It "engulfs" the dreamer and/or R.F.K.; it is aurally similar to the word "execution." The image of "human sewage" identifies the source of this defilement of life as coming from humankind; this was painfully evidenced in both Kennedy killings. The bullets that in reality *rained* through the air are symbolically linked to the precipitation of defecation.

The core of the dream is a condemnation of uncivilized contemporary society. It warns the dreamer that he must find a way to rise above the "human sewage" that threatens to drown or engulf respectability and all that is decent in an assassination of unspeakable defilement.

On another prescient level, the dream may also be symbolic of environmental concerns—the raining of human defecation may refer to humankind's destruction of the world—

the oceans, the rain forest—which, today, is one of Robert F. Kennedy Jr.'s most pressing concerns.

The following prophetic dream was dreamt by **Larry Geller,** hairstylist, friend, and spiritual mentor of Elvis Presley, on the day that Elvis died:

> *At the exact time Elvis was dying I dreamt a horrific nightmare that a groaning monster, a monstrous eight foot Gorilla was chasing me. Every time its claws got close to me I got away. Then I saw Elvis in the clouds, his arms reaching out to help me and I levitated up from the ground away from this monster.*

Dreams that involve being chased indicate that the dreamer feels grounded in a life situation, but more important often symbolize the phonetic meaning of "chaste"—which establishes that the dreamer is of high moral and ethical sensibility. Thus, the dream contains the wish for justification, self-affirmation, and ultimately to be lifted from the darkness. The nightmarish claw of the monster figuratively represents someone wanting a piece of the dreamer. But redemption follows in the symbol of a risen Elvis whose arms or alms (in a phonetic sense) lovingly lift Larry beyond his worldly problems. The levitation is the wish to rise above the heaviness of the moment—running from those members of Presley's entourage who resented Larry's close bond with his friend Elvis.

Viewed as prophetic, the dream reveals Larry's empathic connection to his friend's personal torment and suffering—his timely understanding and perception of Elvis's sense of being driven. For on this level of interpretation Elvis is the one who is chased by his own engorged and monstrous being—with death as his only escape into the weightlessness of clouds. Here, the levitation represents the transformation from the material world to the realm of the metaphysical. Thus, the spiritual content of the dream suggests that Larry has visualized Elvis as both the rescuer (savior) and the one who is rescued (resurrected), and it establishes the wishful belief that Elvis will always be there for those in need.

The following prophetic dream was dreamt by the artist **Ron Ferri** about our mutual friend, Ludovic Autet (see Ludovic Autet's initiation dream), on the day that Ludovic passed away:

> *In my sleep my friend called me. I didn't pick up, the answering machine did. He sounded like he wanted someone to talk to—like calling for help. (I got up at 7 AM to check my machine but there was no message. At 10 PM that night I was informed that my friend had passed away hours after I had walked him home.)*

In that Ron had just spent Thanksgiving with the friend he had just walked home at 5 A.M., the dream indicates that Ron had somehow intuitively sensed something about this friend that had worried him. He may have even sensed that his friend needed help. But because of the lateness of the hour a talk was unrealistic. Therefore, the dream fulfills Ron's wish to have had the talk he already regretted not having, and thus he has his friend call him. "I didn't pick up," is the dreamer chastising himself, and literally means that Ron did not allow himself to act on his intuitive premonition or delve into its prophetic nature.

Interestingly, the telephone usually symbolizes a device that communicates with the dead as it is a receiver that con-

nects one to the other side . . . to distant invisible voices
from far away. As Ron's friend actually died later on in the
day, the dream can be considered one of precognition.

It seems that **Abraham Lincoln** was not just a great president but a seer as well, as he had the following uncanny
dream shortly before he was assassinated. Lincoln had been
up very late, as he was "waiting for important dispatches
from the front," but being weary he fell into a slumber:

*There seemed to be death-like stillness about me. Then
I heard subdued sobs, as if a number of people were
weeping. I thought I left my bed and wandered downstairs. There the silence was broken by the same pitiful
sobbing, but the mourners were invisible. I went from
room to room; no living person was in sight, but the
same mournful sounds of distress met me as I passed
along. It was light in all the rooms; every object was
familiar to me; but where were all the people who were
grieving as if their hearts would break? I was puzzled
and alarmed. What could be the meaning of all this?
Determined to find the cause of a state of things so
mysterious and so shocking, I kept on until I arrived at
the East Room, which I entered. There I met with a
sickening surprise. Before me was a catafalque, on
which rested a corpse wrapped in funeral vestments.
Around it were stationed soldiers who were acting as
guards; and there was a throng of people, some gazing
mournfully upon the corpse, whose face was covered,
others weeping pitifully. "Who is dead in the White
House?" I demanded of one of the soldiers. "The
President" was his answer; "he was killed by an assassin!" Then came a loud burst of grief from the
crowd, which awoke me from my dream. Ward Hill*

Lamon, Recollections of Abraham Lincoln, 1847–1855. *(Nebraska: University of Nebraska Press, 1994). Ed. by Dorothy Teillard*

"Leaving the bed" signifies the willful determination of the dreamer to be active, independent, and definitely vital. The image of wandering downstairs refers to the president's quest to reach a deeper level of conscious awareness (as downstairs is underneath and represents the unconscious). Going from room to room symbolizes a thorough search of his personality, his being. He is suffering someplace within himself, but his suffering is nonpermissive of pity. There is light in all the rooms because there is a revelation—a cry of distress, of puzzlement, and alarm. The dreamer's determination to find the cause of such a mysterious state of affairs shows an analytic mind. As the sun rises in the east, the answer dawns on the president in the East Room: the president is dead, having been killed by an assassin. In a psychoanalytic view, being dead in the White House is the self-referential recrimination and even condemnation of a weary president who felt guilty about falling asleep on the nation. Perhaps he is too old for the job . . . for he is already a corpse. From a paranormal standpoint the dream is nothing but prophetic.

Were these preceding dreams really prophetic, or were they just uncanny coincidences? Were they the midnight musings of intuitive minds—of dreamers who are more finely tuned to what is perceived by others as the random static of the universe? You, the reader, must decide.

33 TYPICAL DREAM MOTIFS

1. Flying Dreams
(see Eva Marie Saint, Pat Boone, Jason Bateman)

2. Falling Dreams
(see David Tang, Denise Richards)

3. Dreams of Climbing Stairs or Mountains
(see Dr. M. T. Mehdi, Jackie Mason)

4. Dreams Where We Are Naked or Insufficiently Dressed
(see Marilyn Monroe)

5. Dreams of Losing Teeth
(see Lisa Gabriele)

6. Love Dreams and Love Visitations
(see Victoria Principal, Soheir Khashoggi)

7. Dreams of Getting Lost or Abandoned
(see Sandra Bullock, Denis Leary)

8. Dreams of Losing Things
(see Hugh D. Auchincloss III)

9. Dreams of Forgetting Things
(see Hugh D. Auchincloss III)

10. Departure or Road Dreams
(see Christopher Cuomo, Andrall E. Pearson)

11. Transportation Dreams
(see Liz Smith, Peter Barton)

12. *Dreams of Visitations From the Deceased*
(see Elvis Presley, Carmen, Daniel Straus, Antonia de Portago, Sir Winston Churchill, Friedrich Nietzsche, Ray Adams)

13. *Dreams of Being Chased by Hostile Forces or Frightening Animals*
(see Bai Ling)

14. *Dreams of Being Shot At*
(see Rita Sever)

15. *Professional Nightmares*
(see Dick Clark, Catherine Hicks, Raoul Felder, Kareem Abdul-Jabbar, Les Paul, Fernando Botero, Joey Reynolds)

16. *Dreams of Being Pregnant*
(see Cyndi Lauper, Allen Ginsberg, Jessica Hecht, Sheila Ryan, Mary Shelley)

17. *Dreams of Losing a Baby During Pregnancy*
(see Madonna)

18. *Sexual Dreams With Erotic Fantasies*
(see Samuel Taylor Coleridge)

19. *New-Identity Dreams*
(see Jacqueline Kennedy Onassis, Abe Vigoda)

20. *Dreams of Not Being Able to Move or Speak*
(see Cameron)

21. *Dreams of Responsibility*
(see John Waite, Judge Philip Maier)

22. *Divorce Dreams*
(see Mai Hallingby, Laura Hunt, Anthony Quinn)

23. *Dreams of Dying*

24. *Dreams of Aliens*

25. *Chess Dreams*
(see Mr. K)

26. *Identity Dreams*

27. *Religious Dreams*
(see Helen Sanders)

28. *Discovery Dreams*
(see Elias Howe)

29. *Dreams of Invisibility*
(see Alexandros)

30. *Cartoon Dreams*

31. *Dreams of Dislocation or Disorientation*

32. *Synecdoche Dreams*

33. *Movie Dreams*
(see June LeBell)

13

Flying Dreams

Flying dreams are the most fun to have, as they empower the dreamer with superman qualities and the sense of omnipotence. They are often dreamt by people who have their feet planted firmly on terra firma—who would like the chance to lift up and drift like a bird, to be less structured and pragmatic, less earthbound. These dreams signify the wish to lighten up, to become unburdened by worries. Most important, these dreams express the need for personal freedom and independence. Flying dreams in men, however, are often attached to sexual excitation because in the act of flying something rises up against the pull of gravity.

The following flying dream was dreamt by one of Alfred Hitchcock's favorite actresses, the cool blonde **Eva Marie Saint:**

> *I'm with strangers, lots of people at a big party. Then, suddenly I'm flying. I take off. I'm looking down. No one misses me. No one sees I'm gone.*

In that *rising up* eludes to the meaning of "uprising" in defiance—and in that *rising up* from the ground is against the natural laws of gravity, dreams of humans flying (and particularly those of children) signify the wish to defy rules and regulations imposed by the adult world. Because Eva Marie Saint was raised, as a Quaker, to feel the burden of the world's suffering, the wish expressed in the dream is to lighten up—to rise above social responsibilities, pressures, and seriousness and go for a romp. Pleasurable flying dreams bring with them the sense of empowerment because they symbolize the dreamer's ability to break from traditions and norms. These dreams often reveal the independent nature of the dreamer.

Flying away from lots of people suggests the need to detach from the herd mentality and maintain one's identity, one's personal space. It also suggests the inevitability of human isolation, even in a crowd, where flying off becomes the "big party"—the consolation and celebration of self-assertion. Taking off may reflect Eva Marie's desire to strip away the societal surface veneers in an attempt to reveal truth and naturalness.

"I'm looking down" reflects the dreamer's humility, for even though fame has elevated her as a star, she is humbled by the realization that no stranger in the crowd misses her or sees that she is gone; this incorporates what is key to performers: the ability to assess others' emotional reactions to them.

The phrase "no one misses me" also serves as a self-justification that it is indeed acceptable to fly off once in a while. It reflects the dreamer's conscientious and dutiful nature, for even though the people at the party are strangers to her she still feels an obligation to her host to be sociable, and therefore she reassures herself that her absence will not be missed.

The following is another wonderful flying dream, of **Pat Boone**'s:

I'm standing in a room. I'm wanting to fly. I'm decid-
ing if I will concentrate hard enough and close my eyes
I'll be able to will myself off the floor. I start small. To
my amazement and happiness I get a few inches off the
floor, first just above tip toe, then gradually I am able
to levitate a foot or two, then up to the ceiling. I begin
to move with more ease and speed, then I go outside
10/15 feet in the air. I begin to swoop and dive and
surprise people.

Flying dreams are empowerment dreams that represent
the wish to emerge from the sheltered interior world of a
child. The ability to levitate to the ceiling, and eventually
beyond, symbolizes the maturational wish to be able to fearlessly approach the outside world. This is the wish to escape
from being under the thumb of watchful parental supervi-
sion. The act of flying represents an alteration of the personality wherein the adult takes the place of the child—in that
levitating is symbolic of this elevation, this (in Pat Boone's
case) ascending to manhood. Whereas going outside the
home suggests a sought-after independence, surprising people with "swoops and dives" shows an awareness of the effect one is having on other people. It symbolizes the
beginnings of social consciousness.

As flying defies the laws of gravity, it symbolizes the defiance of rules and regulations imposed by the adult world.
Thus, Pat unites the infantile aspect of wanting to be able
with the adult awareness that mastery of self can be achieved
through sheer will and determination. A step-by-step transformation of confidence is seen: The dreamer starts small but
gradually realizes his ability to levitate or ascend toward his
upward maturational path to the ceiling. The ceiling poses no

limits as Pat "moves with more ease," goes outside to where he can "swoop and dive" and "surprise people" with his newfound sense of control. Rather than passively being surprised or caught off guard, Pat is the aggressor, the one who surprises, the one who victoriously calls the shots in this coming of age dream that facilitates realization in the dreamer that power comes through having belief in oneself. More than anything else the dream reveals Pat's "amazing" will to succeed.

The next flying dream was dreamt by **Jason Bateman** and is somewhat different from the rest, as he is piloting his own plane:

> *I am flying a plane, or in it. It's a big, huge 747 going slow, almost ground level, flying through trees, under bridges, and around buildings. It's scary, but it always seems to miss things. It's in such slow motion. It misses all these extremely dangerous things it's going through and by.*

As already mentioned, a key element in flying dreams is the wish for empowerment—the freedom to break away from conventional norms, mores, and established ways of thinking so that the dreamer will be able to gain a broader perspective and be unencumbered by the restraints of everyday life.

Whereas being *in* a plane represents the desire to rise above earthly frustrations, *flying* the plane is the wish to make something attainable, to gain back control, establish independence, and span great distances at breakneck speed. But in this dream the plane flies low and is going slow, signifying thwarted intentions. Flying at "almost ground level" represents a fear of going back to square one. The slowness of flight suggests that the dreamer worries over delays and setbacks—perhaps things are not going fast enough for him. Flying through trees, and under bridges represents the convoluted path progress is taking, and shows that Jason is preparing to overcome or circumvent obstacles through his own deft handling and personal maneuvers. Yet by piloting the plane, Jason is also symbolized by the plane that "always seems to miss things." In this view, Jason may feel that life is passing him by too quickly. Therefore, he defensively *makes* the plane slow down. The plane flies through and by dangerous things but never connects or lands, which signifies that the dreamer prefers to remain detached. The dream comforts Jason into believing that as long as he is at the controls he can hold himself back from any "risky business."

14

Falling Dreams

alling dreams are generally liberating in that they are concerned with letting go. They are often dreamt by people who are perceived of as stiff, people who are guarded, who often wish to experience their opposite state of being. These control freaks or perfectionists would love to be able to participate in the game of trust, where they are told to simply fall back, to trust that someone will be there to catch them and prevent them from hitting the ground. But they rely too heavily on themselves and therefore find it difficult to depend on others. The falling dream compensates for the fear of ever really losing control. It symbolizes opening the clenched fist—a child's feeling of abandon without any thoughts of the consequences. Falling dreams can also involve negative feelings of guilt—of having fallen or having become baseless. These dreams can also represent the fear of failure—of falling from the heights to the depths.

David Tang, the brilliant entrepreneur, the CEO of Pacific Cigar Co., founder of The China Club, and Shanghai Tang, had the following dream:

> *I often dream that I'm on a thin ledge of a high building, facing the building, looking down over my shoulder, hanging on by my hands, my fingers, having the*

feeling that I'm going to fall. I fall but then I wake up relieved.

The debonair David Tang finds himself, much like Cary Grant in Hitchcock's *North by Northwest,* in a bone-chilling moment hanging on by his hands to a thin ledge of a high building—this is a dream of high anxiety. But, whereas being on a ledge suggests one is courting disaster by taking chances in life, facing the building in such intimate proximity reveals the desire to identify with strength and structure. Hanging on signifies Tang's determination; hanging by one's fingers symbolizes stretching beyond one's limit, and represents the wish for expansion, extension, and growth.

The dream expresses humility by reflecting upon mortality—allowing oneself to visualize mentally one's worst fear in order to overcome it. Whereas the fall represents the wish to let go, awakening before the crash means that Tang knows he will never hit bottom and reveals his inner faith that he will avert any potential disaster. Looking over one's shoulder symbolizes the wisdom of assessing what has happened in the past.

The actress **Denise Richards** has recurring dreams of falling. The dreams are only remembered in fragments, but the physical sensation of falling is what is most prevalent. Her dream is as follows:

I frequently have a dream where I'm up really really high and I'm falling and I never hit the ground.

Cinematically speaking, Denise Richards's character in the movie *Spaceship Troopers* went "up really really high" in a space vehicle. Her movie may have elicited this particular falling dream. Dreaming of being up symbolizes a buoyant spirit with a positive outlook on life. (Denise was eagerly anticipating the film's release.) Similarly, being up high represents aspiration because the sky's the limit.

But everyone knows how difficult it is to stay on top— particularly in Hollywood. To achieve even a minimum of fame requires tremendous upward striving and a strong belief in one's talents. But one can trip up and make mistakes. Falling from the heights reveals that Denise has anxiety over potential failure or loss of achievement; control is an issue. Yet, paradoxically, falling also reflects the wish to let go, which is why there is an endless falling. The fact that Denise never hits the ground means that she will never hit bottom, or bottom out, because Denise never gets down at all. The dream is frequently repeated because going through the motions of free-falling anxiety is therapeutic experience as Denise learns how to lighten up.

The dream, however, may also reflect something that Denise has had to give up in her life—something that she has let fall by the wayside.

15

Dreams of Climbing Stairs or Mountains

Dreams of climbing up and down stairs or trekking up mountains involve bodily movement and so are frequently associated with sexual activity. (See G. Gordon Liddy's dream.) There are exceptions, however, as in the case of the following dream, which equates movement with work. The dream was dreamt by **Dr. M. T. Mehdi,** the former secretary general of the National Council for Islamic Affairs. It presents the difficult task of ascending a mountain:

> *I am climbing a mountain on the back of an old, tired camel. It is a painful climb, very hard and tiresome. But when I get to the top or almost the top of the mountain, I see another hill ahead of me and will have to collect my strength to start over again, climbing the new mountain. These mountains are either in the barren, dry, hot desert, or coming out of an ocean, surrounded by water from every direction. My climbing is to attain safety; otherwise, I will become dehydrated, suffocated, or drowned. I am determined not to succumb to that fate. Usually, the camel is either a one-eyed beast, or completely blind.*

Dr. Mehdi's anxiety dream over the world condition reflects his role in life, his profession as peacemaker. The "mountains" symbolize the world's seemingly *insurmountable* problems, and Mehdi's aspiration to rise above them. The road is steep, the vehicle (camel) weary, bad-sighted, or blind—something rather than sight is needed to attain safety. Indeed, the "one-eyed" camel needs the inner eye of wisdom to serve as its second. To reach the top of the mountain the "blind" camel needs *blind* faith. Mehdi knows that life is a constant struggle of *ups and downs* . . . exaltations and depressions, and to remain atop the mountain is difficult, for there is always another mountain or hurdle to pass. The symbolic fear of drowning or suffocation is the actual fear of being swallowed by the system. Mehdi fears annihilation by an aggressor that will destroy all traces of existence. Although nature is visualized as the aggressor (producer of flood or drought), it substitutes for mankind, the real annihilator.

The durable camel (Dr. Mehdi) is the *beast of burden* with a heavy responsibility—to save mankind. The dream warns that if world peace is not attained, man will either drown or paradoxically become dehydrated. "Determined" not to have this fate, Mehdi will not be satisfied to reach the top of a mountain, for there will always be others to scale. If vision fails, he will rely on what is more powerful than sight . . . the spirit of faith that guides him on. More than anything else Mehdi's dream is the wish of ascension.

Another example of a dream that involves climbing was dreamt by the comedian **Jackie Mason:**

I run out of the house because the house was on fire. I went into someone else's house to get away from the

*fire. A young woman answers the door. I climb up some
steps and tell her I am here to hide from the fire. But
she knows me and wants me to tell her jokes. I do and
she laughs so hard she cries.*

Once again, dreams that are involved with climbing stairs
or mountains are often related to sexuality, because they depict rhythmic activities. As the sexual act is often a tran-
scending experience the content of the dream should reveal
this transcendence. And it does! As house is often a symbol
for mind, running out of the house is a symbol of getting
away from oneself or one's thoughts. Fire represents heat,
fever, or frenzied activity and also symbolizes a rhythmic
movement. And so, by fleeing fire, which produces smoke
and sucks up oxygen, Jackie is literally trying to give himself
some breathing space. This is the wish to slow down the pace
of a very active mind . . . to go somewhere else, to another
house without a fire.

But the new house contains a fire of another kind, the fire
of desire, as the young woman who opens the door represents
the wish for a sexual encounter. The young woman also establishes that Jackie's foray into the mental realm has been
brief, as he has returned once again to the physical realm—to
things sexual. Although, as we will see, the quick wit, the
clever quips can never fully be left behind in that they are
still required material.

The climbing up steps symbolizes that sexual activity is
occurring. A disguised sexual connotation is revealed when
the young woman knows or recognizes the dreamer as being
a comedian, for she wants him to tell her jokes, which is euphemistic for wanting him to perform. The young woman,
who laughs so hard that she cries, symbolizes sexual satisfac-

tion, as tears are bodily secretions. This is the dreamer's wish for an erotic conquest. The dream also reflects the dreamer's desire to continue his life's work, perhaps at his own ex-pense, to bring happiness to humanity by presenting laughter to the world.

16

Dreams Where We Are Naked or Insufficiently Dressed

reams of nakedness are revelatory in nature, as the dreamers wish that something will be revealed to them. It is a wish for openness—a protest against deception. The dream is also a wish for recognition; the dreamer wants to be noticed on a grand scale. Yet dreams of this sort usually suggest that the dreamer is after retribution, as the dream wants some event or occurrence to be exposed for what it really is. The nakedness represents coming clean, so to speak, and basically states "I have nothing to hide," but the statement is made in a defiant tone with its hands on its hips, as the nakedness is usually a trade-off for what it wants exposed in return.

But dreams of nakedness that replicate our official state of entry into existence also symbolize the desire for rebirth. The dreamer is ready to regress all the way back to the womb, suffer that first slap, and hope for a better start.

Dreams of being insufficiently dressed express something different—like the wish for urban renewal without the cash flow. These dreams reveal or, dare I say, *partially reveal* that the dreamer is not yet ready for full disclosure as he or she lacks decisiveness. In that dreams of being insufficiently dressed also signify a state of dishabille they often reflect the emotional disarray of the personality.

The following dream of becoming naked was dreamt by **Marilyn Monroe:**

> *In this frequent childhood dream I am walking down the aisle of a church, and as the organ thunders out hymns I have the desire to throw off my clothes, the outfit of the orphanage, and stand naked for God and everyone else to see. (Zolotow, New York: Harcourt, Brace & Company, 1960)*

As already mentioned, dreaming of becoming naked is a common theme. But whereas nakedness usually causes embarrassment in dreamers who are afraid of being unmasked or seen in their unadulterated essence, Marilyn's dream produced only pleasurable feelings. This is because Marilyn Monroe did not fear exposure but rather welcomed it, in that being exposed symbolizes being found out—and more than anything else Marilyn wanted to be found. The act of discovery serves as compensation for her orphan's sense of being lost in her environment, as feelings of being unintentionally lost cover the more intolerable sense of being intentionally abandoned.

Marilyn wanted to be exposed so that people would know who she really was. Never knowing her father, and barely knowing her mother, who had been institutionalized during much of Marilyn's childhood, contributed to Marilyn's lack of identity. Thus, Marilyn's dream is a wish fulfillment for *public* recognition, which belied her need for *personal* recognition and sense of self.

Within the dream, God the father has taken the place of her real, elusive father as a means of verifying her existence. Wishing to be seen by God contains the reversal of Marilyn wishing to see her own father—to metaphorically meet her maker. Her wish to be seen naked can be interpreted as the desire to be reborn—minus the orphanage clothing of her old existence—for by shedding her garments of institutionalized anonymity Marilyn is able to transcend her orphan's sense of herself and express her individuality. Yet her wish is carried to the extreme, as Marilyn wants to stand out even among an anonymous group.

Walking down the aisle is an allusion to getting married, and also to being given away. The organ "thunders out" hymns in a manner that manifests Marilyn's hidden anger toward her father, who *gave her up*. Hymn is an aural, phonetic reference to the masculine pronoun. It is no surprise, therefore, that this is the precise moment in which the dreamer chooses to *give herself up*—to throw off her clothes as a means of retribution and vindication . . . as if Marilyn is addressing her father and symbolically saying, "Here, take a good look at what you have given up."

17

Dreams of
Losing Teeth

For men dreams of losing teeth usually symbolize fears of being castrated, particularly when there is more than one tooth involved; these dreams may also represent masturbatory fantasies, as a missing tooth often alludes to a tooth that has been pulled. For women, however, dreams of losing teeth are viewed as compensatory wishes for gain in that physical loss is understood as symbolic of that which has been separated from the body—wherein something has been emitted, as in the birth of a child. The following teeth-losing dreams were dreamt by **Lisa Gabriele,** producer of CBC's *Big Life:*

> *I have this horrific recurring dream that I am in a public place where I am speaking and while I am speaking I have to carefully try to hide the fact that I am spitting out my teeth, one after the other, into a napkin, to the point where all of them are gone.*

As stated, the most typical interpretation of a tooth-losing dream is that the dreamer has the wish to be pregnant, as dreams wherein something emerges or becomes separated from the body usually symbolize the birthing process. As dreams often disguise or substitute regions of the body—

often transposing the lower onto the upper part of the anatomy—the female orifice of the mouth is substituted with another orifice, the vagina.

Carefully having to hide the fact of the teeth loss either represents the desire to hide the bulging stomach of the pregnancy, or to repress the absence of that state. The napkin symbol is closely related to the female sanitary napkin—the receptacle of menstrual blood that signifies the necessity to further negate or hide the truth of the pregnancy. The monthly menstruation is symbolically, if not visually, attached to the napkin image—the soiled napkin states that there was no fertilization this time. The white napkin, of course, symbolizes the desired pregnancy. The white of the teeth that fill up the napkin clarify the impregnation wish.

Lisa's second dental dream is as follows:

> *I've had to have an entire new set of teeth fitted to replace the ones that have fallen out. Basically, I've had to ask the dentist to remove them all and give me a new set, and I've prepared myself, in my dream, psychologically for that.*

Once again, this tooth-obsessed dream may be a birth fantasy, but there are other possible interpretations. For example, this might be an attachment-gone-awry dream, where replacement of what has been lost is of paramount importance. If we substitute the top portion for the bottom portion of the body the dream imagery may signify that the dreamer has lost her footing, as though the rug was pulled out from under her. This may symbolize that her life is in an upheaval. The falling out may also allude to a falling out or severed relationship.

The losing of teeth also represents the loss of identity, as the deceased are frequently identified by their teeth. As opposed to representing birth, the falling out may represent the death of an old self, which necessitates a new set of teeth. For, the loss of teeth signifies that the dreamer has lost her grasp or grip on life, or on reality. In other words, there is no bite left. But within the context of the dream, Lisa wishes to renew her connection with the world, as she is psychologically prepared to undergo a reconstruction that will enable a new presentation, a new persona that will be able to smile once again. The new set of teeth symbolizes the desire to go after a new set of ideals.

Here is another one of Lisa's tooth-losing dreams:

I was chewing gum. I go to take it out and it gets stuck. The cap comes off from my tooth. Underneath the cap there are tiny little nails. The core of my teeth were built of these little nails and I start pulling them out, and wrapped around the nails are tiny wires which I also pull out. I am in Cuba at a Cuban dentist's office. He (the dentist) was absolutely stunned because he had never seen anything like this work. It was intricate dental work. I was afraid that he wouldn't be able to build my teeth back.

This third dream viewed in tandem with the rest indicates that the dreamer is as stuck or fixated on the symbol of losing teeth (childbirth) as the gum that gets caught in her teeth. The cap comes off and for the first time the dreamer is able to expose what is underneath, at the core of both teeth and dream—nails and wires. Although the intricate construction symbolizes the wish to build or create something internally, the nails and wires attempt to ensure that whatever is internal is nailed down and wired shut. The dreamer's conflict is whether or not to become pregnant, wherein the vital wish to become pregnant is compromised by fear and a powerful separation anxiety.

18

Love Dreams and
Love Visitations

FILLING A VOID: A FORM OF WISH FULFILLMENT

Love dreams are valentines—emollients rubbed into the aching muscle of the heart. They occur in three different forms: (1) dreams of broken relationships that wishfully reappear as solid, (2) dreams that seek to pair the dreamer with that special someone, and (3) dreams of visitations from deceased loved ones (see Victoria Principal).

Forms 1 and 2 occur within a psychological framework: In the first form the dreamer rewrites his or her personal script so that a former love interest is incorporated into a typical Hollywood movie-ending replete with sunset. The dreamer brings back a loved one for emotional nourishment—the refrigerator is empty and the unconscious mind is hungry. In the second form the dreamer is faced with repressed thoughts wherein the love instinct is often made known in terms of conflicted desires—the dreamer who (in consciousness) is either unable or unwilling to consciously express any tender or romantic thoughts toward a certain individual suddenly experiences a change or revelation of heart within the action of the dream.

Whereas form 3 is known to occur in the realm of the psychological wherein the wish is one of reparation or self-consolation, it is also thought by many (spiritualists and occultists included) to occur within a paranormal framework wherein the living dreaming mind (or receiver) is viewed as a perfect vehicle for the deceased to enter . . . much in the same way as a radio frequency is picked up from far away.

Many love dreams (form 2) have also been interpreted as manifestations of paranormal phenomena wherein the dreamer (as receiver) is enabled to pick up the thoughts of an admirer (as sender). In this instance the admirer (as sender) has infiltrated the dreamer's (receiver's) unconscious mind through either willful, meditative, or directive thinking. The unrepressed and uninhibited dreamer (receiver) has unknowingly opened the window of the dreamworld and allowed to enter an admirer who has knowingly or unknowingly infiltrated the dreamer's unconscious mind. Of course this can happen in the reverse wherein the dreamer is the sender . . . longing to lure in a loved one for a captivating dream tryst.

It may be better to have loved and lost than never to have loved at all, but this in no way makes it any easier to deal with the loss of a loved one, which is why there are so many dreams in this genre. For even after long periods of mourning, the loss of a loved one leaves an indelible void, a hollow feeling of emptiness that the mind often fills by fitting the loved one into its missing, heart-shaped, jigsaw space—for the dreaming unconscious wants closure or completion. Dreams that offer another glimpse of the deceased make available the opportunity for communicative interaction through dream narration, which in turn evokes a moment of resolution that brings comfort and peace to the dreamers. But the question remains . . . are these visitations real or have they been manufactured by the dreamers as a coping strat-

egy, a protective measure in an effort to fill the gaping hole of
loneliness and loss?

The following, then, is either an authentic love visitation
(in the sense of the paranormal) wherein the deceased Andy
Gibb actually revisited his ex-lover **Victoria Principal** while
she was sleeping for the express purpose of comforting her
with words that needed to be said, *or* a dream that Victoria
Principal gifted herself with in the hopes of soothing her raw
emotions and ridding herself of any residual guilt. You decide!

> *In that we had never again spoken after the break-up,
> during my dream Andy came to me because he knew
> that I was haunted by this and we sat down and had the
> talk that I wanted to have, and we needed to have, and I
> thought it was so much like Andy to come back and do
> this. (VH 1)*

When a loved one suddenly dies there is always remorse
over words that were left unsaid, conversations that were
never had. And because the mind and heart demand closure,
the dream process inevitably delivers . . . by serving up a
visitation wherein the deceased is brought back for the explicit purpose of settling unfinished business. In other words,
this visitation is a wish fulfillment wherein the dreamer gifts
herself with the presence of her loved one in a defensive attempt to end a melancholia that has persisted.

Victoria endows Andy with a thoughtful selflessness that
he was incapable of revealing while drugged and alive (for
given Victoria's ultimatum, ''It's either me or drugs,'' Andy
chose the latter). Thus, she rewrites the event by making
Andy comply with her need to talk (which he never had the

time or inclination to do in reality). The dream phrase, "we sat down and had the talk," represents Victoria's strong need for communication—as sitting down to talk usually symbolizes a pivotal time in a memorable relationship between two people. (Note: Seated at a round table indicates an intimate and agreeable relationship whereas seated at a square table suggests a relationship fraught with difficulty.) Victoria projects onto Andy her own want and need to be comforted, as she includes him (by the use of the plural pronoun) in their need to talk.

Yet on a metaphysical level of interpretation, there is the distinct possibility that the deceased may find the unconscious mind an accessible vehicle of entrance. As previously stated, when the unconscious mind has stripped away all of the distractions and stimuli that the conscious mind is subject to, the sleeping mind on such occasion may be in proper form to act as both transmitter and receiver, much like a radio that is able to pick up unknown distant frequencies.

LOVE VISITATIONS

It cannot be overstated that love visitations are the most sought-after dreams because they reunite the dreamer with a deceased loved one—particularly in cases of sudden deaths wherein the dream alters time and makes possible the expression of feelings that had not yet been revealed and words that had not yet been uttered. For it is the purpose of the visitation dream to pave the way to emotional closure. But the visitation dream has another important function. It allows an ongoing communication with the deceased that eliminates the sense of futility and finality, and ultimately death.

Dreaming of a deceased person reflects the wish for continuance, as it confers upon the dreamer a sense of immortality. For in most narratives, these dreams proclaim that *no one dies—they just disappear from view.* The dream suggests that the world of consciousness is at odds with the internal psyche (soul) or essence of the personality that is invisible apart from its fleshy exterior, the material body. The dream confirms that this immaterial essence is still a reachable, viable consciousness in the workings of the unconscious mind. Thus, the dream consoles our consciousness while stroking our emotional skins, as it forms a reassuring image of the hereafter and its constituents.

The dream concretizes an idea through the visualization of an image that the unconscious mind already knows or has foreknowledge of on some level of awareness—an idea that the conscious mind is not yet aware of. The dream seeks to inform by presenting unconscious insights to consciousness. But consciousness is what gets in the way of recognition. Therefore, we must never underestimate the intellect of the unconscious—the power of its skills. Nor must we dismiss the dream that broadens the boundaries of an unknown framework in the wish to integrate not just consciousness with unconsciousness but mortality with immortality. The following is an example of a consolation dream that contains gratifying conceptions of life in the hereafter:

> *My driver (who was deceased for one year) was walking toward me down the street conversing with an older man. He smiled and said Hello. He looked wonderful. He handed me my handbag. I had lost my bag and he had found it for me.*

There is conversation and communication after death, as symbolized by the two men conversing. The banality of the situation is generated by the casualness of the conversation. There is movement and activity as opposed to stasis in that the two men are walking—there is upright mobility. There is communion with others and therefore camaraderie. Happiness is conveyed by a smile, hardiness by the driver looking wonderful. There is stability, as the two men are on the street. An aura of omnipotent wisdom is achieved, as the driver has found what was not visually available—the missing handbag. He has given the emptiness of space a material dimension. By giving back the handbag the driver represents beneficence and a well-meaning orientation. The symbolic intention of returning a lost handbag is that it reissues the identity of the recipient, as a handbag symbolizes the sense of self—the individual persona. Thus, the dead are not to be mourned, as they are not the ones who are lost—we are. But, perhaps we can be found in our dreams!

Synopsis of Consolation and Reassurance

- In reality: Driver is both loser (of life) and object lost.
- In the dream: Driver is both finder and object found. He finds the dreamer (in the symbolic form of her handbag); he is found in that the dreamer encounters him.
- Translation: The dead are not lost but found. They give back what is taken away.

Here is another example of a consoling visitation dream that was recently dreamt by **Soheir Khashoggi,** the aunt of Dodi Fayed, several months after his tragic death:

Dodi and I are outside walking in the street. He is holding my hand. It is dusk. He is telling me that he is fine, and very much in love with Diana.

In order to interpret a dream it is most important to notice the way in which the dream was worded, the narrative structure, the way it was told. For example: The dream phraseology "Dodi and I are outside" is very different from "I was with Dodi outside." The meanings of both are inherently the same, but in the first (the version within the narrative text of the dream) a definite connection is expressed. "Dodi and I" expresses the wish for connection. In addition, in the first version the word "outside" is kept away from Dodi's name—it follows after the word "are"—as outside represents the detachment of the world of the deceased, which is outside of the realm of the living. The second (nondream) version connects Dodi with outside.

The wish for connection is continued, as Dodi is holding Soheir's hand. The holding of hands symbolically establishes a link like a daisy chain—they are together, now and forever. Even though this is a happy dream visitation, the symbol of dusk reveals Soheir's continual mourning. The consolation comes from Dodi expressing his well-being and his love for Diana. Once again, the dream is either a wish fulfillment of the grieving Soheir to commune with her beloved nephew, or a genuine visitation from the world of the deceased. The answer, unfortunately, cannot be concretized within the pages of this book.

Another type of love visitation dream often contains a warning and is thus thought of as protective in nature. But whether the dreamer is unconsciously aware of a danger that is repressed in conscious life, or whether, in a paranormal sense, the deceased has purposefully returned to warn the dreamer is a matter of conjecture.

A woman named M had two consecutive visitation dreams in one night. What is highly unusual is that the visitations were from two deceased individuals: one, a former lover, the other, her brother's trusted friend. The first dream is as follows:

> *I was in a house with no furniture. Everything is bare, empty. There are green leaves all over and foliage like in a jungle. I hear a bell ring. I go out the back way to see who is there. Two men are outside. They come into the house. One is a servant, the other is my old boyfriend. We go into the back yard. I see birds with sharp beaks. The birds are talking. The two men take pictures of the flying birds. They come to the dining room. My boys are there on the left side. The servant had given my old boyfriend two sticks like Popsicle sticks. He says they are plane tickets for me to leave with him. He says we have to use them in 365 days. I say what about the children. He says the children cannot go.*

Being in a house with no furniture symbolizes the emptiness of the dreamer's life and the bleakness of her situation. But the exterior has a jungle atmosphere that suggests that the dreamer is in the thick of it—entangled and entwined in some wild and dangerous involvement. The leaves all over—in the phonetic rendering of the word—are visual signs or messages that the dreamer must leave her home, her situation. Hearing the bell ring is yet another auditory message—a presage, an omen—and can signify a recognition: a bell went off. Going out of the house the back way suggests there is reason for furtiveness. The men who come into the house are deceased souls entering the dreamer's unconscious domain. Pictures of flying birds are also visual presentations that are given to the dreamer—flying birds symbolize airplanes and serve as an additional hint that the dreamer must vacate by flying away.

M's boys are on the left side because they are to be left behind in the world of the living. M is handed two sticks by her deceased lover; the sticks are substitutes for plane tickets that must be used in one year's time and indicate the imperative nature of the departure—and the danger involved. The sticks are also symbolic jolts or pokes meant to stimulate awareness, to motivate and mobilize the dreamer into taking action.

The second dream wherein the dreamer meets a deceased friend is of a similar nature:

I visit my old country house. My brother's friend is there, but there is no food in the house. We walk the sidewalks to a bakery. We sit at a table. I have a credit card in one pocket, but no money. He has no money either. We cannot just sit and talk so we have to leave. He goes outside and up a long stairway. He says, "Follow me. We go order." I say, "No."

Whereas the first house had no furniture, the second house has no food, symbolizing that M is not being nourished, or given sustenance; as food is the staff of life the dream bears ill tidings. The brother's friend is M's spirit guide who tries to sweeten the situation by finding a bakery. M credits herself as being a good friend, but without money she is viewed as powerless. A conversation is attempted but because there is no money the two have to leave, which expresses the same sense of urgency—that departure is mandatory. The deceased friend goes up a long stairway and asks M to follow, which is echoic of her former dream—instead of flying away M is asked to ascend a stairway.

When viewed within the context of the dream, the haltingly simple "we go order" is more than truncated grammar, as it clearly states, "We must go. This is an order." Yet although this phrase is an implicit warning that M must leave, she says no, revealing an inner conflict.

Taken together, these dreams make M aware of what she has been repressing—the desperate wish to change her present life situation, to leave her troubled world behind. (Here, it is necessary to mention that at the time of both dreams an ex-boyfriend of M's had come to this country without any money, job, or hope. He had sought her out, and moved in with her. His attachment was most unwanted, as he immediately assumed the role of boyfriend; in his depressed state he became jealous of any rivals to the point where he began monitoring her beeper. M felt threatened by her ex-boyfriend and even suspected him capable of violence toward both herself and her children. Therefore, she was afraid to take action against him, to throw him out, change her locks, or call the police.)

With this information in mind, both dreams succeed in revealing M's mixed feelings about getting rid of her former boyfriend, in that he is a fellow countryman and someone she had come to fear. This is why in the second dream she does not attempt to follow her brother's friend up the staircase, for what is unknown or unseen is perceived as frightening. Yet, both dreams clearly indicate the sense of urgency she feels to depart from her home.

From a psychoanalytic standpoint, these dreams have a perfect narrative fit. In other words, they make sense, as they reflect the situational anxiety and emotional turmoil of the dreamer. Viewed as actual visitation dreams, the two deceased beings have entered M's dream world as spirit guides in an attempt to warn her of impending danger.

If nothing else, these dreams involving deceased beings— with their flagrant signs and omens—provide a strong case for giving visitation dreams the benefit of a paranormal interpretation along with a psychoanalytic one.

19

Dreams of Getting
Lost or Abandoned

Dreams of getting lost or abandoned basically stem from feelings of insecurity and a loss of identity. This form of anxiety dream also indicates a dependency in a regressive sense, where the dreamer is longing to feel loved, protected, and nurtured. These dreams may also result from feelings of inadequacy and self-doubt. Yet dreams wherein one is abandoned may actually reveal the projected wish of the dreamer to be the one who abandons. The following anxiety dream was dreamt by **Sandra Bullock:**

I am in a Range Rover. In the front are two friends. In the back, I am sitting with Warren Beatty and Annette Bening. The car pulls up at this really trendy restaurant. I don't want to be there . . . it's the kind of restaurant where everyone looks at one another. But my friends say it is going to be great. Inside, it's huge and everyone is dressed in leather vests, gold chains and jeans. For some reason, Warren, Annette and one of my friends stay in the car. The other friend goes to the restaurant's bathroom. I sit there and sit there. Sweating. Freaking out. Two hours later I go into the bathroom to find my friend, but the friend is gone. They've all left me there. Angry. I leave the restaurant. I go in

> *the parking lot and they aren't there.* (As reported in *Us,* February 1997)

Sandra's success has placed her in an expensive vehicle whose front and back seats delineate the division between the celebrity world and the world of the general public. Although Sandra is in the "back" in the world of the stars, the dream reveals her anxiety about her future role in Hollywood. It is a rough world and the road to enduring fame is paved in rugged terrain that necessitates the vehicle of choice—a Range Rover. Yet Sandra seems to be taking a back seat to the ordering of her life, to the demands being put upon her. By not being up front or in the driver's seat it is obvious that Sandra is driven and that determination and constancy will be needed, as the dream makes clear how rapidly seating arrangements can change.

Sandra not only fears being abandoned or forgotten by Hollywood but also by the false friends that fame serves up on its golden platter, the friends that ultimately leave her lonely and disenchanted, with an angry feeling of being betrayed. The friends that convince Sandra that the restaurant will be great are the ones that desert her. The huge and impersonal restaurant becomes a place to get lost in—a drop-off point as Sandra finds herself all alone. Sandra goes to the bathroom more as a cleansing experience than to look for her lost friend, as the restaurant symbolizes the desire for nourishment of another kind. Nonetheless, going into the parking lot suggests Sandra's desire to park, to find a spot for herself within the trendy and fickle Hollywood heart, even if she has to go it alone.

Denis Leary's dream indicates that he is lost in that he dreams he is going in the opposite direction of where he wants to go. His dream is as follows:

> *It's me and Madonna in the back seat of a NYC taxi. She turns to me and says, "Will you breast feed my baby?" Before I can say no, the driver shouts out "I will!" The driver turns to face us—it's Al Roker. Suddenly the cab screeches to a halt and I find myself standing on the corner of 1st Ave. & Ninth St., my old neighborhood. A bus pulls up and the doors swoosh open. The driver says "Goin' Uptown?" I look up. The driver is Jenny McCarthy.*

This dream, with its taxi and bus symbolism, reflects transportation and movement, particularly the moving from downtown to uptown, suggesting how far Denis has come from his old neighborhood on Ninth Street. That the dream takes place within the taxi symbolizes the length of the journey and the contentment on the part of the dreamer to be within the confines of a celebrity world, as the taxi is peopled with Madonna and Al Roker. Mr. Roker, as the highly recognizable weatherman, may represent the weather itself (a powerful element in nature), as he is the driving force that takes Denis back home. But the weather blowing hot or cold can be your best friend or worst enemy, signifying the uncertainty and variability of life. Therefore, the taxi driving downtown represents a fear of regression.

Yet the dreamer, not wanting to go farther downtown, dispels this fear when the cab suddenly screeches to a halt. A bus pulls up and welcomes Denis to ride uptown back to the glamorous world of celebrities, as symbolized by Jenny Mc-Carthy, the bus driver who invitingly "swooshes open" her doors in a sexually suggestive manner. (This dream seems a fine example of how a dreamer can literally *change the direction* of the way a dream is going by sheer will.)

Being with Madonna in the back seat is a sexually charged image that sets the tone for her strange request of asking Denis to breast-feed her baby. By reversal, this means that Denis wants Madonna to breast-feed him; by displacing Madonna onto the baby, Denis wants to breast-feed the baby—it seems Mr. Leary has in mind some other method of oral satisfaction—perhaps the concealed wish to substitute the breast for the male organ.

In that Madonna also symbolizes the mother of all mothers, the core of the dream is the wish to be protected and nurtured, which is thematically consistent with the dream motif of getting lost or abandoned; the cab that abandons Denis in his old neighborhood necessitates his being rescued by another mother figure, Jenny McCarthy, who "opens" her doors in symbolic representation of the nurturing womb within.

20

Dreams of Losing Things

D reams of losing things are frequently tied to feelings of loss of control, as the objects lost are irretrievable. Material objects are often associated with our sense of worth as they are viewed as extensions of ourselves. Thus, the object lost would signify a personal loss. But with each lost object the meaning is different. For example, a female's dream of losing her handbag would symbolize a grave loss of personal identity in that a woman is represented by what she carries with her: her makeup, mirror, comb, wallet, credit cards, driver's license, etc. It may also represent a loss of sexual identity, as a handbag is a receptacle in which things are put. But a lost umbrella would mean something totally different—the fear of not being covered or protected. The loss of a bathing suit would reflect the wish for liberation.

Yet these dreams are often associated with feelings of being violated, where something is taken from the dreamer against his or her will. The following dream was dreamt by **Hugh D. Auchincloss III:**

I dreamt I was swimming in heavy surf, caught by a big wave and then swept out in undertow. I even lost my bathing suit, and was shy about getting back to the beach. (It was mid morning.) All of a sudden a beauti-

ful mermaid came to my rescue (although the water had calmed and the waves had decreased), but she rode the undertow, and attached to her hair was a string of seaweed with my bathing suit attached, so I was saved from embarrassment!

This dream is all about letting go and allowing oneself to be swept away. It represents the wish for total abandon and reveals the youthful exuberance and adventurous spunk of the dreamer. There is the desire to cross boundaries, to make accessible what is inaccessible to an ordinary regulated man. Thus, the lost suit playfully reemerges attached to the hair of a mythic mermaid.

Losing a bathing suit is like throwing one's inhibitions to the wind; it also reveals the need to strip one's life down to its bare essentials, to be exposed to the primacy of the moment. The big wave may be viewed as a visual rendering of salutation—a symbol of recognition that comfortably draws one in. But the big wave is tinged with the excitement of the unexpected: the beautiful mermaid. This is Jung's anima, the female in male consciousness—guide and goddess of divine intervention who metaphorically allows Mr. Auchincloss to safely emerge from the deep waters. The intention of the quest is not to find the lost bathing suit, which surfaces like a revelation from the murky depths of the unconscious, but rather to recognize the value of the stripping away of artifice and complicacy.

21

Dreams of Forgetting Things

reams of forgetting things are intentional as they have certain value for the dreamer. Remembering Allen Ginsberg's anxiety dream wherein he forgets his plane ticket we are reminded that the wish of the dream was to forestall the journey that represented departure or death. Once again the object that is forgotten is meaningful to the interpretation. Hence, a forgotten ticket which has departure stamped all over it, holds a different meaning from that of a forgotten fruit; a forgotten fruit may represent the wish to deny oneself the sensual pleasures of life, or the wish to ignore one's accomplishments. The following is another dream of **Hugh D. Auchincloss III:**

> *I often dream of forgetting my datebook, or of looking for it and not being able to find it.*

Dreams of forgetting and mislaying an object are usually tied to intentional forgetting; however, the intention may stem from a variety of meanings. In that a datebook records days and hours of appointments, it symbolizes the passage of time—and specifically memory. Necessarily, certain dates are tied to circumstances one no longer wants to recall, to painful memories one wishes to have stricken from the record, and to certain future dates that one would like to avoid if one feels conflicted or put upon.

But dreams of forgetting that evoke annoyance or anxiety in the dreamer take on practical or sentimental value, as an importance has been placed on the object mislayed, such that forgetting a datebook may reveal the sadness of no longer being able to contact those one wishes to and may reflect concern about fulfilling obligations and commitments, thus underscoring the conscientious nature of Mr. Auchincloss. In this view the lost datebook, still symbolizing the passage of time, evokes the anxiety of forgetting good memories. Yet the mislaid datebook may be a symbolic sacrifice where the dreamer trades pages of his past in order to ward off some other unpleasant memory; it may also represent a defiant stand against keeping one's final rendezvous with destiny and suggest a desire to transcend time. Looking for the datebook suggests that the dreamer ponders what the future holds in store for him.

22

Departure or Road Dreams

Departure or road dreams often represent the dreamer on the quest of discovery and can be termed the "easy rider" of dreams. They are about the journey of life in the Jack Kerouac fashion. Therefore one does not find in these the kind of anxiety present in dreams involving departures or journeys that signify death. These dreams are about living and learning along the way about one's personal freedom and independence. The following road dream was dreamt by **Christopher Cuomo:**

> *I'm on a motorcycle going around a curve. I swerve to avoid hitting a truck and I crash off the road onto the grass. When I get up to see what has happened I see another motorcycle coming into the same situation. I try to run up there to tell the guy, to warn him, but I can't run fast because my clothing is heavy. Instead, he runs off the road and smacks into me knocking me back up on the motorcycle onto the road again. I look back to see what happened to that guy, to see how I got into the jam, and I see the same series of events that made me crash in the first place.*

As a road dream generally represents freedom of expression, the mode of transport often defines the individual on his journey of exploration. Christopher is defined by the masculine symbol of a motorcycle: powerful, forceful, revved up, and full of drive. When thrown a curve, Christopher knows how to maneuver his bike to swerve from the obstacles life puts in our paths—for even when he crashes he is on soft ground. But he will not be kept down for long as his resilient and tenacious spirit forces him to get up to see what has happened.

The guy on the other motorcycle "coming into the same situation" whom Christopher tries to warn is none other than himself. But as this second crash cannot be avoided, Christopher is knocked back up onto his bike. This crash makes an impact or lasting impression in that Christopher learns how to deal with consequences: he learns to accept the past as something that he cannot change. But there is an epiphany in looking back, as Christopher is able "to see the series of events" that conspired to bring about his downfall. This is the realization of what history has already shown us—that if we do not learn from the past we will repeat our mistakes ad infinitum.

The following departure dream was dreamt by **Andrall E. Pearson,** CEO of PepsiCo:

Leaving a train station I cannot find a cab. I'm in a hurry so the pressure is on the search. But somehow I cannot find a cab to get to my destination.

Whereas "leaving a train station" means that the dreamer is aware that he has gone most of the distance, "not finding a cab" reveals there is still more ground to be covered. As Pearson is standing out in the street, his thwarted departure may represent an outstanding venture, unfinished business, a deal not yet done. For this is a dream of frustration where things do not fall into place. Yet, with no cab to be found, one thing is sure: Pearson is not taking the easy way out. Implicit is the awareness of life's realities, the fear that one will not be able to meet one's obligations or beat time's perpetual clock.

Andrall's forestalled arrival home means the journey is viewed as more important than the destination. Thus, "the pressure is on the search," or quest, the clues picked up along the way that are valued more than what is eventually found. Reaching a destination means establishing a fixed end point and stasis; not arriving at an appointed destination reflects a liberated spirit—the wish for spontaneity and continuance.

23

Transportation Dreams

The theme of transportation crops up frequently in dreams and is symbolic of movement and ceaseless activity. The dreams often symbolize the drive of the dreamer, or that the dreamer is driven. The following transportation dream was dreamt by the award-winning columnist, **Liz Smith:**

> I am waiting, of course, for a friend who does not seem to mind keeping me waiting. While waiting for her a in a big car, a Lincoln or Cadillac, I decide I'll take a short cut to picking her up. I drive the car down one of those old fashioned subway entrances and then up the stairs with the intent of—what? Getting on the tracks? All I know is the car gets stuck. I leap out of it and rush back to the street with the intention of instantly returning with help to extricate it. When I get back, with no help, the car is gone. I talk to several old fashioned subway working types, men in suspenders, looking puzzled and annoyed, who try to help me trace the car. But I don't find it. Later, I'm in the car and every time I come up on people, the brakes fail so that though I have slowed down, I still bump into people. I am exasperated at the brake failure but can't seem to remember the brakes are bad until the next person is in front of me and I am unable to stop.

A car often symbolizes one's place in the world—the bigger the car the more expansive the space. The friend Liz anxiously waits to meet is herself, as she drives the car down, underground, in an attempt to reach a deeper level of understanding—the unconscious below the surface. But there is never enough time, which is why her car transforms into a subway—a subterranean way of getting back on track fast. But as there are no short cuts to personal revelations, the car gets stuck or sidelined. The dreamer stops dead in her tracks, her train of thought derailed.

Liz surfaces with the noble intent of returning once again to the depths of self-discovery. But the car is gone, as there is no more time for introspection. The dream continues above ground with Liz in the car full of drive and ready for action. The brakes fail because as a gossip columnist bumping into people represents social contact. Being unable to stop suggests a frenetic lifestyle; there is no time to put on the brakes, for there is always someone out in front and more ground to cover—another story, another deadline.

The following dream involving transportation was dreamt by the actor **Peter Barton:**

> *I'm driving a car. It's windy. There's dangerous debris, tree branches all over the road. I'm maneuvering around the obstacles without stopping, almost like a video game. Suddenly, the dream switches to a sexual encounter with a female acquaintance I don't really like. Against my better judgment, I give in to her advances.*

This form of transportation dream places the dreamer in a dangerous situation, for the dream represents a need for spiritual release similar to an initiation experience where the hero, the driving force, who is driving the car, must achieve a goal or reach a higher level by passing impediments along the way. Peter's character in the dream is being maneuvered by the detached dreamer who is at the controls, playing life's ultimate video game. Avoiding dangerous debris establishes a meandering pattern that reveals psychic growth, or a realization of a personality in the process of becoming. The debris symbolizes whatever has become detached; similarly, the tree branches represent the offshoots that are no longer attached to the tree, thus alluding to an evolution, or perhaps a psychological maturation and representing the wish for individuation—to become free of something constraining. At breakneck speed Peter succeeds at "maneuvering around the obstacles without stopping," when the dream suddenly halts and switches to another location. This indicates that a rest is needed for a moment of calm reflection.

The physical encounter with dangerous debris switches to the sexual encounter with a female acquaintance, presented as another obstacle the dreamer must overcome on the road to achievement. Yet the dreamer gives in to her advances against his better judgment, for as the girl advances, Peter necessarily withdraws from his movement, his progression forward. His drive is momentarily halted. But in that the dreamer is self-reproachful the dream assures that he will be on his way in no time.

24

Dreams of Visitations from the Deceased

Dreams of visitations from the deceased are the most satisfying and usually the most profound dreams, as messages are usually passed along—advice, reassurance, or consolation is given. Often the dreamers awaken with a sense of awe, or just a general feeling of happiness. These dreams are wishes to send and to receive communication from beyond the mundane world of the living. They reestablish faith in the hereafter, as they offer the assurance of continuance. Most important, they present the idea that no one ever dies. The following visitation dream was dreamt by **Elvis Presley,** whose twin, Jesse, was stillborn at birth (as told to Larry Geller, personal hairstylist, spiritual mentor, and close friend of Elvis, at Graceland):

> *I had this dream that The Presley Brothers were performing. My twin brother Jesse and I were on stage, both wearing white jumpsuits with guitars slung around our shoulders. He was the spitting image of me except he could sing better.*

As losing a twin can produce what is called survivor's guilt in the twin who remains, it is not surprising that Elvis would dream of sharing the incredible phenomenon of his fame and even his talent with his stillborn brother Jesse. What is interesting, however, is that Elvis endows his brother with a better singing voice than himself, and this is what brings spiritual meaning to the dream, the implication being that the brother's voice is coming from another place, with heavenly timber, tone, and resonance.

Teaming up with one who has passed to the other side reveals the wish to be elevated to a higher level of existence, which is symbolized by the stage. The guitars around the shoulders may represent symbolic wings or angelic equipment, as this is an angelic scene from above—with singing voices, stringed instruments, and the color white representing spiritual wisdom and purity. Taken literally, the image of jumpsuits suggests that these are suits that jump or rise. Thus, the dream underscores Elvis's spiritual quest, as it reveals his wish to become one with a heavenly being or presence, to join with his twin other side to become whole and thereby enlightened.

The following visitation dream was dreamt by the very beautiful **Carmen,** supermodel:

> *It is winter. I am sitting on a park bench in the park with my father (who is deceased). There is a blanket around us, so we are not cold. My father tells me, "you will be all right."*

As a concert violinist Carmen's father would frequently leave home to perform, leaving Carmen to await their many wonderful walks in Central Park upon his return. By filling the park with the warmth of her father's presence and the warmth of childhood memories, Carmen's dream reverses the chill and bareness of winter—the season of leaving—for the wish of the dream is to reunite with her deceased father and gain consolation from this reunion.

Even in winter there is warmth between father and daughter—a blanket is around them. The blanket represents security and comfort and reflects the wish to be taken care of—tucked in—covered and protected. As the blanket is another symbol for the father, Carmen is blanketed in love.

Sitting means it is not yet time to go; to park means to stay in one spot. Poignantly, being benched means not allowed to play—Carmen's way of making sure that her father will not leave her as he did in the past to play the violin. The park bench symbolizes solidity and permanence, offering the reassurance of her father's words, ''you will be all right,'' as if to say, I am here with you always.

Daniel Straus, the CEO of Multicare, had the following visitation dream:

> *My father appeared to me after his death, before I started Multicare. I couldn't reach him. He was saying something to me but I couldn't hear him. He called my name. It was in an underground parking garage.*

Something underground, below or beneath the surface, usually represents the unconscious, because it cannot be seen from above. Thus, Straus's unconscious is trying to come to terms with his father's death, his father's absence, or invisibility. The underground parking garage symbolizes a graveyard where his father is not buried but rather garaged as a parked car; in that cars are only parked temporarily, his father may again resurface, or resurrect. The car also represents the future vehicle of the journey to the other side, which animates and vivifies that which has come to a halt.

Daniel's determination to reach the unobtainable shows tenacity and willfulness. In a wish to communicate with his father for consolation Straus has his father call out his name. The name-calling is significant, an important symbol of recognition that makes whole again the dreamer's newly fragmented sense of identity, as pieces of self often chip away with the death of a loved one. Necessarily, Straus neither hears nor understands what his father has said before, because only the name Daniel is meaningful in that it has the restorative power of self-validation.

A most amazing and touching visitation dream was dreamt by a friend of mine, **Antonia de Portago:**

> *I am in the Parisian house I was raised in. I am told by my mother's friend my mother will call me on the telephone. This shocks me, since I am aware my mother died long ago. I stay next to the telephone, awaiting my mother's call. I ask my late mother's friend for my mother's telephone number, so I may call her myself. The friend's response hurts me. She says my mother doesn't want me to know where she is, even though she is still alive. I ask her friend to tell me where she is, or to take me to her, but to no avail. I try to call her anyway. When we speak, she tells me she is not dead after all, but is in hiding because she doesn't want any part in life anymore, and she doesn't want anyone to know she is alive, or where she is. She just wants to be left alone. I ask to see her; I can't wait to run to her and fall in her arms, but she refuses . . . even after I beg her, crying, to let me see her.*

The dreamer wishes to speak to her deceased mother, and by reversal, dreams her mother wants to call her. The telephone, as a symbol of communication—of wanting to be connected with someone—conveys a voice from far away over invisible wires. The telephone, which bridges the unseen/inaccessible with the accessible, gives rise to associations with those that have passed to the other side.

''Mother's call'' can mean mother's telephone call, or, figuratively, an aural beckoning to return home, which may reflect the dreamer's depressive notion to reunite with her deceased mother through dying. As is the case when a parent dies, children often feel responsible—that they have done something wrong to deserve abandonment. This engenders feelings of guilt. Thus, Antonia punishes herself by dreaming that her mother wants no part of her—as she does not want her daughter knowing her whereabouts.

Being told her mother is alive is a wish fulfillment. Wishing to be taken to her mother is again the depressive desire to join with the mother. When the mother, who previously did not want anyone to know she was alive, finally does the right thing and speaks to the dreamer, the mother makes it known that she is making an exception with Antonia, which has the effect of consoling Antonia's hard feelings, as she is made to feel special.

Although the dream denies the dreamer from ''running to her mother, and falling in her arms,'' which would affirm the life instinct within the dreamer, thoughts of abandonment and rejection are indulged, in that the dreamer deliberately dreams of a mother unwilling to reunite with her child. This indulgence in rejection allows the dreamer to feel self-pity, which plays an important role in exonerating her guilt. The mother is the bad one, the one who hurts the feelings of the child. Thus, the dream ends positively with the dream's self-reconciliation and the expression of anger toward her mother for having died. In other words, the dream rids the dreamer of a guilt she may have been carrying all these years.

The following is a visitation dream wherein the dreamer's deceased grandfather and step-grandmother are able to reassure the dreamer that the anxiety she is feeling prior to the dream is unjustified:

> *I am at a party. The party may be taking place on a boat. There are lots of people all around. To the left is a bar where I notice my grandfather (who is deceased) nonchalantly holding a cocktail in his hand. Then my step-grandmother appears. She comes over to me smiling, happy to see me. I say, "you look wonderful." And then I ask her how she is. She says everything is just fine.*

When asked about what preceded this dream the dreamer related that she had been concerned over a boat cruise that her son would be taking the following night. As the cruise was sponsored by the International Cigar Society, the dreamer had envisioned that the boat would be filled with smoke. This thought gave way to a more troubling one: the turgid smoke would most probably make her son (a non-smoker) leave the smoke-filled interior for a stroll on the deck where he could enjoy the fresh air. There might be crowds of people on deck and by some misfortune her son might get inadvertently pushed overboard. After relaying these thoughts, the dreamer freely admitted that her worry seemed unnecessary yet she still felt ill at ease, until she had the above dream, which had the effect of calming her jittery nerves.

It must be mentioned that the dreamer's grandfather was

always called by his initials, I. G., and that the step-grand-mother's name was Connie. For, during interpretation of the dream, as the dreamer put the initials of the two names together she was amazed to come up with C. I. G. (an immediately perceived reference to cigar). Then the dreamer reflected that the party in the dream may have been on a boat. Lastly, the dreamer was able to recount that the deceased couple was entirely at ease and that her step-grandmother spoke the following words: "Everything is just fine." This was ample reassurance that all would be OK.

Indeed, the following night the son went on the cruise as planned and, as predicted, remained on deck for most of the cruise; he had a charming if noneventful evening. Thus, the visitation dream may be interpreted as the dreamer's way of calming her anxiety, yet another example of how the unconscious mind deals with everyday stressors. In other words, as mentioned earlier, *the dream is the coping response.*

A most unusual visitation dream was dreamt by a friend's grandmother nearly two years after the death of his grandmother's husband. His grandmother had been mourning day and night, crying regularly as part of what had become an obsessive melancholia, until she dreamt this particularly vivid dream:

My deceased husband was standing in a rapidly growing pool of water. It was raining tears. He angrily shouted out to me, "Stop it, Evanthia. You are drowning me with your tears." As he said this, and as the water level was rising to the point where he could have literally drowned, a column fell which he embraced. He was trying to save himself from drowning.

Horrified over the vision in her dream, the dreamer no longer cried, and thus ended her long period of mourning for her deceased husband. The dream was therefore therapeutic in nature, as it relieved the dreamer's melancholia, it allowed her to stop grieving and crying without any feelings of guilt. In fact, the act of not crying was now perceived to benefit her deceased husband, who would otherwise drown in her tears. For the rising pool of water symbolized that the dreamer had literally cried buckets, that she had cried assiduously.

Taken as a true visitation—as a paranormal phenomenon—the wish of the deceased husband was to put an end to his wife's habitual suffering. The only way this consolation could be accomplished was for the deceased to visually show his wife how her tears were harming him.

The following visitation dream was dreamt by **Sir Winston Churchill** while he was attempting to paint a portrait of his father, who suddenly appeared, seated in Winston's big red leather armchair in the artist's studio. However, in conferring with his grandson, Winston Churchill, I was informed that this dream of Sir Winston's was generally thought to be a reverie, or that which occurred when Sir Winston was in a tracelike state. I was also informed that no record exists of Sir Winston ever having painted a portrait of his late father. This fact is insignificant, though, in that Sir Winston has revealed that the moment his father vanished he was too tired from the vividness of the illusion to continue painting. Therefore, the painting may never have been completed. Sir Winston was urged by his children, Randolph and Sarah, to write down the dream, which, in its written form seems an elaboration of the original dream or fantasy. Randolph Churchill has said the dream was most uncharacteristic of his fa-

ther's writings. Herein follows the gist of the dream—mostly
paraphrased and greatly truncated:

"I was painting in my studio." I had been sent a badly
torn canvas portrait of my father, (Lord Randolph). "I
thought I would try to make a copy of it. My easel was
under a strong daylight lamp . . . On the right of it
stood the portrait I was copying, . . . behind me
. . . a large looking-glass" from which I could examine "the painting in reverse. I must have painted for
an hour and a half, . . . deeply concentrated on my
subject. I was drawing my father's face, gazing at the
portrait," and turning round "to check progress in the
mirror . . . My mind was freed from all other
thoughts except the impressions of that loved and hon-
oured face . . . on the canvas, . . . the picture,
[and] in the mirror, I was just trying to give the twirl to
his moustache when . . . I turned round . . . and
there, sitting in my . . . upright armchair, was my father . . . just as I had seen him in his prime . . .
'Papa!' I said." My father asked me to fill him in on
what had transpired over the years. (A long conversation ensues where Lord Randolph hears his son recite
the history of the 20th century while ironically leaving
out the one thing that would have amazed his father the
most—that Winston had become prime minister during
the most crucial period of his nation's history—that he
had rescued his country and perhaps Western civiliza-
tion in the process. What is strange, then, is that Randolph has stated that this dream or fantasy of his
father's was probably inspired by Winston's regret
that his father would never learn of his great achievement. But if this is so, why did Winston refrain from
mentioning it?) The father ends the conversation, say-

*ing among other things—that he never expected that
Winston would have developed "so far and so fully"—
that Winston should have gone into politics where he
might "even have made a name for [himself]." The
father gives Winston "a benignant smile," strikes a
match to light his cigarette, and in that "tiny flash,"
vanishes. Made tired by the illusion Winston notes that
he cannot continue his painting—his "cigar had gone
out, and the ash had fallen among all the paints."*

The "torn" canvas portrait of Winston's father symbolizes that the *fabric* of memory is coming undone—therefore,
Winston tries to improve his memory, "to make a copy of
it" in order to keep his father's image alive in his mind's eye.
"Drawing" his father's face represents the wish to *pull forth*
the paternal persona. Studying the painting "in reverse"
suggests that Winston wishes that his father were alive—that
things would be seen as they are today. *(Winston, having
only been twenty years old when his father died had not yet
come into his own as he had done badly in school. His father
often wondered what would become of him.)* The "mirror"
behind Winston represents the desire to examine the past.

Winston's father returns "in his prime" at thirty-seven
years old—Winston is a seventy year old man. In answering
all of his father's questions it is now Winston who is the instructor, the teacher, the knowledgeable one, which is perhaps why he modestly withholds the revelation of his
personal success. The motivation behind Winston's most cu-
rious ellipsis seems to be that Winston did not feel himself
worthy of competing with his father—for indeed his great
achievements far exceed those of his father. It also seems
certain that Winston would not have wanted to intimidate his

father, but would rather have remained somewhat mediocre in his father's eyes so as to retain the closeness that he felt toward him in his early years.

When Lord Randolph vanishes Winston is too tired to continue painting. For the painting of the father is the physical expression of the male illusion. Winston cannot sustain the illusion; his "cigar had gone out"—the male energy was depleted. The culmination is the ash—the end of the fire— perhaps the sad realization that Winston could not, even in fantasy, praise his own accomplishments.

The ash is the reality of death, which has momentarily mixed with the tools of creation as represented by the paints. The ash is dry, the paints are wet. The ash is the father's ashes, which have fallen among the paints, the reality of the father's death momentarily blots out Winston's creative spirit.

The following dream is one that may be termed an indirect visitation wherein the dreamer views from afar the reemergence of his deceased father stepping out from the grave. In 1849, several months after the tragic event of his father's funeral, **Friedrich Nietzsche,** five and a half years old, had the following dream:

I heard organ tones as at a funeral. As I saw what the cause seemed to be, a grave opened up suddenly and my father climbed out of it in his burial clothes. He hurried into the church and [came]shortly out again with a child under his arm. The grave [opened,]he [climbed] in and the cover [sank] back onto the opening. At the same time the organ tones fell silent and I awoke. (From Carl Pletsche's *Young Nietzsche,* New York; The Free Press, 1991)

In this frightening nightmare the wish is clear—for Nietzsche to join his father. The father is viewed as omnipotent in that he is seen willfully coming and going from his own grave. This is meant to reassure the dreamer that death can be opened up or penetrated, that it is not a fixed state of existence but rather one of choice. The grave opening symbolizes that the entrance to the world of the deceased can be broken into.

The father hurrying out from the church with a child under his arm, as though he has stolen it, reflects the loss of Nietzsche's childhood. Indeed, the father is symbolically viewed as robbing Nietzsche of his childhood joys.

Yet on the day following Friedrich's dream, his younger brother, Joseph, died and was buried in the same coffin as his father—placed in his father's arms. One now has to reexamine young Nietzsche's dream. One can say that the dream was prophetic without altering the idea that Nietzsche's secret wish was to remain with and be protected by his father—the child carried out by the father in the dream is literally carried off under his wing.

The dream may also be viewed as a fulfilled wish of Nietzsche's to remove his only male competitor from the Nietzsche household—for his younger brother Joseph's death would make Nietzsche the only male in the household. What is more probable, however, is that Nietzsche suffered from feelings of abandonment and lovelessness, which would have made him dream of his brother being taken by his father as the object of his father's affection and devotion.

At the end of Nietzche's dream "the organ tones fell silent" which symbolizes that the music has stopped in young Nietzsche's life. When he says, "I awoke," it seems a sad realization—as if to say that he awoke to the miseries of life, the sudden departures that leave one with feelings of loneliness and longing. Early on in the dream when Nietzsche says, "I saw what the cause seemed to be," he may have been speaking about his own suffering and the negativity surrounding love, human weakness and dependency, the hardship of mourning attached to the love of the departed.

The following visitation dream was dreamt by **Ray Adams,** a descendant of John Adams and John Quincy Adams. At the time the dream occurred Mr. Adams had been mourning the tragic death of a friend who had just been murdered on the island of Mustique:

I was in this darkly exotic room. It was a party atmosphere with anonymous people moving in and out. There was really no conversation and my deceased friend Suzy was flitting about. She was moving or just leaving for somewhere. She came into the room with an armful of small boxes—gifts—and she put them in my lap. She said, "I want you to have these." I opened up some of the boxes. There were two Dupont pens and some chocolates. Then she gave me another box of bittersweet chocolates from Paris that looked like sushi. Suzy was dressed all in black and now seated on the lap of my friend Max. He was all in black as well. She had on a bouffant skirt that completely covered her legs and where she was sitting. They looked so happy that I wanted to take a photo and when I turned to get the camera—she was gone.

As a room symbolizes the dreamer's persona—Ray incorporates his deceased friend into his room—as she was physically described as being "darkly exotic." The anonymous in and out movement of people represents the ebb and flow of life, living and dying. There is no conversation—words cannot convey the dreamer's sense of loss, which the dream remedies by the deceased bringing gifts. Gifts signify an element of mystery, as they have to be unwrapped in order for their contents to be known; they represent the dreamer wishing to uncover the facts behind his friend's murder. Yet gifts also represent the material world, something solid to remember his friend by. The gift of the pens symbolizes the need to communicate or correspond with the deceased; the two pens indicate the wish to both send and receive.

Suzy flits about as she is no longer grounded in reality, but rather leaving for somewhere undefined. Her "bouffant" skirt covers where she is sitting and hides her legs, which minimizes the importance of walking and hints at another kind of mobility—perhaps she glides or flies.

The sushi chocolates are edible symbols of Suzy and the wish to internalize or commune in the religious sense with her spirit. The photo that never gets taken is the sad realization of the dreamer that he will never be able to retain or immortalize the image of his late friend. The memories—like the chocolate—are bittersweet.

25

Dreams of Being Chased by Hostile Forces or Frightening Animals

D reams of being chased often signify that the dreamers are trying to reaffirm their moral and ethical values, as the word "chased" has the phonetic rendering of *chaste*. But the hostile forces or frightening animals may often represents one's own inner demons. The following anxiety dream was dreamt by the actress, **Bai Ling:**

> *I am running in a forest, being chased by wild animals . . . lions, tigers, and leopards. They are growling at me, very loud. I am out of breath. Their growling becomes loud, frightening music. At the end of the forest the ocean is dark and angry. I feel trapped but then I see a high, delicate tower that I climb. As I am looking down at the animals at the base, the animals are now small and cute, the music, peaceful. The ocean is a calm blue. It matches the sky, and there is a peaceful mist. The sun is shining. Everything is warm and glowing. I am no longer scared but since the animals are beginning to climb up, I realize I can't stay here. I fly off and feel a sense of peaceful weightlessness.*

With wild animals in hot pursuit in the background, a dark and angry ocean in the foreground, air filled with growling noises and frightening music (a symbol for angry voices) the dream environment depicts a world of confrontation, or more specifically, a hostile country that the dreamer feels trapped in. Being part of this country, Bai Ling assumes part of its beastly anger, as she is on common ground with the lions, tigers, and leopards. Yet she finds a way to subdue this anger and to rise above the animal world. For the ''high, delicate tower'' that elevates Bai Ling symbolizes her self, standing tall, apart from the herd mentality, which indicates that she has found a higher resolve—a towering strength that sets her apart from the rabble of the crowds.

But the dreamer knows that the more removed one is from a situation, the more distant and impersonal it becomes, the less frightening it seems—as exemplified by the animals that now seem ''small and cute.'' The mist is viewed as peaceful because it is emotionally protected—it blurs the jagged edges of reality and dulls what is actually sharp and painful. In that the phonetic rendering of the word ''mist'' is *missed,* the symbol also represents that which has been intentionally overlooked or repressed. For, as we shall see, security is only tenuous. When the animals begin their climb up the delicate tower, the dreamer realizes that she cannot stay. (In reality, Bai Ling is exiled from her homeland in China.) As flying in dreams represents ultimate freedom, a freedom beyond restrictions and societal restraints, the dreamer flies off feeling a peaceful weightlessness. An emotional burden has been lifted—perhaps Bai Ling's dream makes the sad realization that she can never go home again.

26

Dreams of
Being Shot At

Dreams of being shot at often reflect a sense of being victimized, persecuted, or violated. Dreams of getting knocked down often represent the wish to show the world that these dreamers can weather any storm and rise to the occasion, as these dreamers never die but always get back on their feet. Thus, these dreams are usually self-affirming in spite of the negative imagery. The following dream was dreamt by **Rita Sever,** the charming hostess of NBC's *Friday Night:*

> *I was walking down the street near my house when*
> *someone came from behind a tree and started shooting*
> *at me. I drop down, but then I get up, and as I get up*
> *the shooting starts again. I drop down once more, and*
> *then I get up again.*

On the surface Rita's dream may appear a bit ominous, yet on closer look it is actually a self-affirmation dream similar in meaning to the Broadway musical *Fiddler on the Roof,* for both dream and play espouse the optimistic ideal: If you fall, you must pick yourself up and start anew. Similarly, Rita will not be stopped in her tracks, or blocked from her chosen path in life; she will gamely continue. As Rita gets up she meets challenges head on. Thus, the dream can be viewed as a statement of Rita's perseverance, strength, and courage, as it symbolizes not letting life bring you down.

Nothing can harm Rita's indestructible vitality. No one can keep Rita down or stifle her will to succeed as she rises to every occasion, for Rita is too strong allow negativity to shoot the air out of her tires. The repetitious up-and-down movement in the dream represents life's vicissitudes and underscores the dreamer's basic hardiness of character and spirit, for one must be able to duck from the glancing blows of existence and withstand setbacks. In other words, sometimes one has to take a step backward in order to move forward. Above all else, Rita is a survivor.

The danger behind the tree represents that which is hidden from view. And even though the tree is ahead of Rita, the shooting comes from behind the tree, which indicates that the dreamer has repressed a past anxiety that may emerge or sneak up on her sometime in the future when she is off her guard and least expecting it. (This is the return of the repressed from the unconscious.) Yet by acting out this fear, the dreamer proves that she will be able to meet this challenge head on and survive intact.

27

Professional Nightmares

THE ACTOR'S NIGHTMARE: FORGETTING LINES

The typical actor's nightmare involves the forgetting of lines, the changing of scripts, the mislaid costume, or any other event that would serve to ruin a performance. The anxiety is over not being able to perform, to face public scrutiny. But more important, the dream recognizes that acting is a gift and the fear is that the gift will be taken away, that the dreamers will forget how to do what they excel at. The following actor's recurring nightmare was dreamt by the perennial master of ceremonies, **Dick Clark:**

> *I have to appear in a musical that is well known and has been running for a long while. But I have never seen the show. I've heard none of the music and haven't seen the script. I am saying, "at least, show me the script," but I have to go out in front of a large audience totally unprepared.*

This dream presents the typical anxiety frequently experienced by performers, because of the demanding task of putting themselves under the public spotlight, and this kind of dream is often dreamt before some such appearance is about to take place. Anxiety dreams are often caused by the fear that one may be caught off guard or unprepared, yet these dreams may also arise from expecting a danger and/or preparing for it, even though it may be an unknown one. Therefore, an anxiety dream of this sort often reflects a conscientiousness on the part of the dreamer to be ready for any eventuality (not just a performance) and is often dreamt when the dreamer feels the burden of some existing responsibility. The dream reflects the dreamer's wish to meet what is expected of him (indicating a responsible and dutiful nature). Thus, this recurring anxiety dream may be seen as a form of defense that recurs in order to bring the dreamer back to the situation he fears so he may master it and not be taken unawares.

Interestingly, this dream involves a philosophical questioning and contains, perhaps, the concealed wish to achieve a higher understanding of life. When the dreamer adamantly says, ''at least, show me the script,'' he is in effect saying, let me know what part I play in life. This also signifies the dreamer's desire to look ahead into the future, to metaphorically see how the play ends. Stepping onto a stage is the desire for self-presentation but also symbolically means that the dreamer is aspiring to another level of awareness, a higher realm of the unknown that one is never quite prepared for and is thus apprehensive of. The large audience may symbolize the awesome presence of an eternal being and restates the anxiety of not being prepared for the unknown and/or the world beyond.

The following actor's nightmare was dreamt by the actress **Catherine Hicks:**

*I am in an opera, with scenes and songs. I am an actor
and the costumes are sparkling all different colors. I
know that the number they are doing now on stage is
the one before mine but I do not remember my lines
and I can't find the stage manager to give me the
script—it's all very dark and I'm running around the
corridors backstage behind heavy velvet curtains . . .
I wake up right before I go on stage.*

Once again, this is a typical actor's anxiety dream similar
to that of Mr. Clark's, where the fear of forgetting one's lines
is of paramount importance. And once again there is a deeper
philosophical level to the dream. As an opera often symbolizes life's situations with its Sturm und Drang, its passion
and its spectacle, Catherine, as an actor, is questioning what
part she plays, what purpose she serves in existence. The
scenes are the facades that we encounter; the costumes are
the roles that we assume, the guile and trappings that cover
our nakedness—the truth of who we really are. But Catherine's costumes "sparkle all different colors," which suggests that she embraces life in general—the many walks of
life—and is awed by the vivacity and excitement of the experience. Wanting to see the script is all about control, as it is
the wish to see into the future to know what is waiting ahead.
The stage manager symbolizes an omnipotent god.

The corridors that are backstage represent the unconscious, as they are "behind heavy velvet curtains," which
may symbolize the unfathomable dark folds of the mind in
which Catherine is searching for answers.

THE LAWYER'S NIGHTMARE: FORGETTING
EVIDENCE

The lawyer's nightmare is another production of the dream world, which deals with the anxiety of losing one's skills. One's talent or one's training must be guarded conscientiously. To the extent that the dreamers realize their talent, such is the degree of fear that it will be stripped away without warning. This is the control element of the dream. For while the dreamers are in touch with their skills, they are in full control.

The following nightmare was dreamt by **Raoul Felder,** a lawyer famous for winning:

> *I begin my windup. I take the witness through events of the recent past, nudging him, guiding him to the corner from which there is no escape, to a denouement. The witness is confident, self-assured. "So, Mr. Witness, you say you would never sign such a document. Well, then, how do you explain THIS?" Time stands still, breaths are held, and a number of necks crane forward. With a flourish, I reach into my briefcase to extract the damning document. Nothing! Frantically my hand plunges into every corner of the briefcase. Nothing! I turn the briefcase upside down and shake it. Nothing! Then I hear laughter.*

This lawyer's nightmare represents the typical anxiety frequently experienced by lawyers whose success depends on being perfectly briefed and prepared, and upon their "damning" skills—where information is the weapon of choice. But as law is the process of revealing truths, Raoul's dream becomes part of the process. For Raoul himself is on trial, being watched by his own witness. The witness watches Raoul "wind up" like the rote mechanical movements of a toy. But Raoul is at home in the courtroom playing cat and mouse—as long as the cheese is clearly in his hands. Although baited and cornered the witness is awaiting a final resolution, it never comes, because finality is frightening. A reversal occurs instead whereby the briefcase that symbolizes a philosophy of ideas, is turned upside down. Views are shaken. The wheel has turned; the dreamer/lawyer is now the mouse in the hands of the witness. Plunging into every corner of the briefcase for the missing document is Felder's wish to submerge his noncombative self that can never surface in the courtroom.

As the witness, Raoul is confident that the lawyer will find nothing. This is Raoul baiting Raoul, Raoul testing his own expertise. But proof, like faith in oneself, need not be seen, and answers need not be given.

Although finding nothing is a fearful prospect, the dream ends with laughter as a form of nervous relief. Nothing is found because the wish of the dreamer is not to condemn or damn but rather to affirm. This is where the dream establishes its more philosophical level of interpretation—proof or evidence is not needed because faith reigns supreme.

THE ATHLETE'S NIGHTMARE: BODY FALLING APART

Nightmares typical of famous athletes usually reveal anxiety over the functioning of their bodies—for the body is viewed as a precious instrument, a Stradivarius violin that must be kept away from moisture for fear it will warp. In terms of importance the body precedes the mind to such an extent that the dreams concern themselves with an anxiety over the maintenance of the physical as opposed to the mental realm.

An athlete's body is a temple, his or her livelihood. It is what sets the athlete aside from anyone else. The athlete's body is performance based, and there is a lot of money riding on that performance. The following athlete's nightmare was dreamt by **Kareem Abdul-Jabbar:**

> *I was home and I jumped into my body. I looked at my body directly and it was falling apart. I had an alarming feeling. I was looking inside my foot.*

In that an athlete's greatest fear is the nonfunctioning or disintegration of the body, this is a typical athlete's nightmare, for Kareem's body, as a symbol of his physical world, is falling apart. But as Kareem is retired he is able to see beyond his athletic career, and thus, beyond his body. Yet to get beyond his body he must view it directly from within, for his cerebral self wants to reintegrate with his physical self. Thus, jumping inside his body depicts the mind/body split. In the past, Kareem jumped to make his patented sky hook, seeking to score; now he makes that leap of faith inside himself—*swish*—seeking harmony and wholeness. Kareem is on a quest of self-discovery, for someone takes something apart to show how it is put together.

Jumping into his body, Kareem takes the basketball cliché of staying within himself a little further, to another level. He shoots for self-critical evaluation or assessment: the dreamer knows that the answers are within himself. The dream is impressive in that it reveals Kareem's philosophical need to understand the cerebral along with the physical nature of things, to gain realizations no matter how alarming they may seem.

THE MUSICIAN'S NIGHTMARE: FORGETTING HOW TO PLAY

The most common musician's nightmare is one wherein the correct musical sound is not produced. A drummer will forget his sense of rhythm or beat, or forget when to use the high hat, or worse—the resounding resonance of his base drum will intone where it is not supposed to, and everyone will notice! A pianist will forget the remaining notes of a concerto, or he may forget entirely how to move his fingers across the keyboard. The gist of the anxiety dream is that the musician forgets how to play his instrument, and thus, how to perform. As performance is not only related to one's sense of self-worth but is also related to one's earning power, the dream serves to remind the musician how indebted he is to his individual talents.

The following musician's nightmare was dreamt by the guitarist **Les Paul:**

I got up to play. I couldn't play a note no matter how hard I tried. I would strike and miss it.

A dream that sets up a chaotic event where an exceptional artist loses mastery over specific talents or performing skills usually pertains to control issues or crises of confidence. Therefore, the usually pleasant action of getting up to play, which reflects positive motivation, becomes stressful as the unexpected occurs; the majestic guitarist cannot play a note. Les's heart attack necessitated that he lay off playing the guitar, and especially performing. Feeling besieged by societal demands, Les's decreased performance schedule led to an increase in performance anxiety, which manifested itself in his dream. But as stress is an active process of fighting back, Les strikes and misses and tries very hard in a conscientious and persistent effort to restore his playing powers, his dependability. The striking means Les is striking out against adversity, fear of failure, and feelings of vulnerability to life's inconsistencies. Similarly, as strike symbolically means will not accept, this is Les's determination to meet the curves life throws him. To strike and miss suggests that adjustments in an old lifestyle must be made.

On another level, the dream may agonize over a childhood experience, as getting up to play symbolizes a child's favorite activity, wherein he is free to express himself. The frustration that ensues when a child cannot have his way or cannot accomplish a goal no matter how hard he tries, frequently produces an act of aggression. In this scenario the child may hit or strike out while often missing the target of his anger.

THE ARTIST'S NIGHTMARE: FORGETTING HOW TO PAINT, DREAMING THAT ONE'S PAINTINGS ARE MISSING

An artist's nightmare is based on the fear that his or her God-given gift will dissipate. Some artists have had dreams of going blind, of having arthritic hands or hands that shake; others have had dreams that depict viewers laughing at their work. Then there are those artists who suffer separation anxiety in regard to their paintings—for paintings are creations, like children, and represent a part of the artist. The following artist's nightmare belongs to **Fernando Botero:**

In reality, I have five big studios. But in a recurring nightmare "I get to my studio and I don't see any of my paintings. House painters are painting the walls. I ask them what they are doing, and where are my paintings. They say the paintings were sold and now this is a shop, an office, or a company. They don't really know."

As one of the great painters of the twentieth century, Botero has dreamt a typical artist's nightmare: he is anxious about protecting and maintaining his artistic talent and the product of that talent. The studio is a representation of the painter himself—the walls that are painted or covered over symbolize the fear that the depth of genius will be replaced by a surface veneer. Botero's *originality* will be substituted for the house painters' *uniformity*. The phrase, "I don't see any of my paintings," indicates that Botero's paintings are not *seen* but rather *envisioned*—and reveals that the artistic process comes from within the creative unconscious.

Dreaming of sold paintings symbolizes detachment anxiety from his work as all Botero is left with are bare walls; Botero as the inspirational part of each canvas has been robbed of his essence. The dreamer is mystified by the derivation of the wondrous creative spirit—no one really knows where it comes from and therefore where it goes.

The Spanish painter **Lluis Lleo** has dreamt another form of artist's nightmare, which expresses the fear of lack of recognition. His dream is as follows:

I leave home and get into the subway. Suddenly I find out that from the waist down I am naked and feel very strange. I'm naked but nobody notices this. I'm the only one. I have no way to cover myself because nothing from the waist up is usable so I guess I have to be naked. But people don't even look at me. I am shy and really uncomfortable yet I persist in having this strange feeling about the people. They're not looking at me. I see them but they cannot see me. I am naked and nobody has noticed!

Lluis Lleo's dream clearly expresses the fear that his artistic genius will go unnoticed. His nakedness "from the waist down" exposes his genitalia—man's means to procreate—but remains unseen. The act of being naked is the wish to reveal and exhibit Lleo's creative ability, but the wish is conflicted and thus thwarted—"nobody has noticed." Perhaps not being seen protects Lluis from another fear—public scrutiny. Lluis may yet be uncomfortable receiving any criticism, good or bad.

THE COMEDIAN'S NIGHTMARE

The comedian's nightmare usually expresses the fear of performance anxiety, of not being able to make people laugh. The following dream was dreamt by WOR's syndicated radio-show host **Joey Reynolds:**

Johnny Carson is on stage performing. He had grey hair as this was during the later years. No one was laughing so I ran to rescue him. They kept booing him. I felt terrible. I was telling him things. I was encouraging him to go on. I didn't want anyone to see me. I said, "try this, this works." I was giving him material.

In this work-related dream, Johnny is a substitute for Joey. Empathy aside, this is why Joey says "*I* felt terrible." The dream deals constructively with performance anxiety— Joey is worried that at some point he will no longer be able to entertain an audience with his glib repartee. Thus, the dream attempts to rescue the dreamer from a grey period in his life, from the merciless and judgmental societal boos and recriminations, from a time when Joey does not want to be publicly seen but would rather remain on the sidelines hidden from view.

But the dream is self-affirming as Joey basically encourages himself to go on—the dream reassures Joey that he has material to spare—and that even the best comics sometimes draw a blank. The rescue motif often symbolizes the desire for rebirth or a career change.

Dreams of Being Pregnant

Pregnancy dreams have many different manifestations. The most common pregnancy dreams are those dreamt by women who are pregnant, burdened by the weight of another life growing inside of them and by the responsibility that this other life engenders. Many pregnant women find it difficult to adjust to the physical change in their appearance.

The birth process necessarily involves the death of the old self—the death of the old lifestyle and its routines—for the baby immediately turns the female into a mother, an awesome transformation to be sure. Yet by becoming a mother the female is placed at the head of the "generational train," which carries with it the sad and frightening realization that the female is no longer a child. The focus is on responsibility, maturity, selflessness, and nurturing, because the female is now the caretaker. Bringing life into this world is wondrous enough; placing that life before your own is a sobering and nerveracking prospect that often materializes in dreams that portray the death of the baby (see Madonna's dream).

Pregnancy makes one reevaluate one's sense of competency. It makes one ponder one's physical limitations or deficiencies—is the expectant mother ready to take care of another being, to nurture and protect someone totally dependent. What if the baby is accidentally dropped? Will this cause irrevocable damage? To insure the fact that no harm will come to one's offspring, some pregnant women have actually dreamt of giving birth to dolls or other unbreakable objects! (See Cyndi Lauper's dream.)

In rare cases, a man will dream of becoming pregnant. These dreams may symbolize the desire to fill a void in one's life, or may represent another form of creation, the creative process, the desire to create, to produce. These dreams may be viewed as a cry against emptiness, a compensation, a wish fulfillment of hope and expansiveness.

Pregnancy dreams dreamt by men are often associated with rescuing someone. They may be viewed as rescue fantasies in that the mother—as the one who births—is generally viewed as the rescuer. These are dreams wherein the dreamers want to leave something of themselves to posterity—perhaps an artistic creation, a body of work, a legacy wherein the creative work is viewed as an heir—as a way of being remembered, as a way of extending their own mortality. Dreams of this sort may symbolize a compensation for the sense of physical limitation or deficiency (see Allen Ginsberg's dream in this chapter). Therefore, in the dream world writer's block may sometimes present itself symbolically as the death of a child in that artistic creations are often viewed as children (see Mary Shelley's dream).

Dreams of being pregnant dreamt by non–pregnant women usually represent the wish to become pregnant, or are a way of affirming a positive sense of self. They represent blooming, burgeoning forth, and progression. Depressions based on inactivity or boredom may resolve themselves in dreams of pregnancy. Pregnancy dreams are viewed as self-affirmations wherein the dreamer is fulfilled and her sense of worth expanded.

Even when work is viewed as a suitable sublimation for pregnancy a dream may emerge "belly up" in an attempt to dismiss the negative, restrictive, and guilt-ridden view that society places on a physiologically fit female wherein starting a family is valued more than starting a career (see Jessica Hecht's dream).

To be rescued from the water is symbolic of birth or rebirth, as the mother is viewed as the rescuer. These dreams reveal the wish to start over again—to become, to find satisfaction, to feel the voluptuousness of life, the sensuality. These dreams are a wish against emptiness, as they are dreams of responsibility.

There are fathers who dream of their unmarried daughters becoming pregnant. These dreams are fathers' wishes that their daughters fill a void in their empty lives—whether through birth or occupation—to find satisfaction and personal fulfillment, meaning and purpose.

The following pregnancy dream was dreamt by **Cyndi Lauper:**

I was around other women who were about to give birth and I was very pregnant. The women around me went into labor and had multiple births. But when I went into labor I gave birth to Mr. Bill. When I tried again I gave birth to Gumby. There was a woman next to me assisting me telling me that I wasn't ready yet and this was a relief obviously because who the heck would want to give birth to a Mr. Bill or Gumby for that matter.

Cyndi had this anxiety dream after she came home from her first class of the Bradley Method of birthing techniques where the teacher had been demonstrating the birth method with a doll. It is not unusual, therefore, that Cyndi dreamt that she gave birth to a doll. However, because dolls represent that which is make-believe, it should not be overlooked that they offer solace in that they eliminate the fears and worries of having to deal with the needs of a real live baby.

Since expectant mothers are often anxious about the well-being of their babies, they often dream of their readiness, or lack thereof, to assume the responsible role of caretaker. Cyndi reassures herself that she will be able to cope with the rigorous demands of motherhood by visualizing other women effortlessly and successfully having multiple births, but is self-critical at the same time—calling into question her own capability as all she begets is a doll. As dolls like Gumby are made of soft, pliable, stretchy clay, they are safe to handle and, most important, unbreakable and "immortal." This is the wish that Cyndi's baby will be hardy and indestructible. "I wasn't ready yet" expresses Cyndi's doubt that she is mature enough for the mothering experience, or ready to give up being a child herself, as she is still playing with dolls. But this inevitably reveals the sincere motherly concern of the dreamer who has been diligently practicing her lessons even in sleep to make sure that everything comes out all right.

The following pregnancy dream was dreamt by **Allen Ginsberg** one week before he died. The actual bulge in his stomach was a result of cancer. The dream reflects Allen's altruistic thoughts regarding the well-being of his life partner, Peter Orlovsky. Allen's remarkable last dream is as follows:

There was a bulge in my right side, this dream recently—just now I realize I had a baby, full grown that came out of my right abdomen while I in hospital with dangerous hepatitis C. I lay there awhile, wondering what to do, half grateful, half apprehensive. It'll need milk, it'll need exercise, taken out into fresh air with baby carriage. Peter there sympathetic, he'll help me, bent over my bed, kissed me, happy a child to care for. What compassion he has. Reassured I felt the miracle was in Peter's reliable hands—but gee what if he began drinking again? No this'll keep him straight. How care for a baby, what can I do? [Allen's dream will be included in his forthcoming Death and Fame: Poems 1993–1997.]*

This dream was dreamt the day before Allen Ginsberg was diagnosed with terminal cancer, one week before he died. Being hospitalized with hepatitis C had made Allen dream of surviving. Thus, the wish fulfillment of this last dream reveals Allen's anxiety over being hospitalized and turns a dangerous life-threatening situation into a happy event. A fear of death is supplanted by a miraculous birth in that the bulge on Allen's right side is reassuringly diagnosed as a full-grown baby. This way the dreamer is only "half apprehensive"—the apprehension countered by his grateful feelings.

The dream suggests that Allen was intuitively aware that his death was imminent, as the dream attempts to tie loose ends, to look for solutions: Allen imaginatively fills the projected void his absence will leave in the life of his significant other by giving Peter a child to care for. His worry over Peter drinking again is squelched as he reassures himself that this child will keep Peter straight. The dream reveals Allen's empathic spirit, his humanity, and his sympathetic nature.

In that dreams of pregnancy are associated with the creative process, the baby may represent Allen's poetry, his body of work, his creation, which he will leave in Peter's reliable hands.

The following dream was dreamt by the actress, **Jessica Hecht,** who was *not pregnant* at the time of the dream and was, in fact, about to premiere in her starring role in Broadway's *The Last Night of Ballyhoo:*

> *I suddenly have this terrible pain in my abdomen, a realization I am pregnant. My family offers advice. My sister takes me to a health food store to buy all these remedies, advising me to have an abortion, when this sweet girl at the counter who was checking me out grabs me and says, "You're not pregnant. You're O.K. You don't need anything." I had a realization she was right, this angel. I looked back and the girl was no longer there.*

Jessica's "terrible pain in the abdomen" expresses a strong need. The pregnancy realization suggests this is a coming of age dream, as something wishes to be born. A void or emptiness must be filled. The pregnancy situation gains the attention of family members who offer rather than give advice, indicating there are strings attached. Solutions are sought in the form of remedies that must be bought and paid for at a health food store. But, whereas food symbolizes nourishment, the remedies clearly refer to corrective behavior under parental rules or guidance as Jessica is symbolically advised to have an abortion. In other words, she is asked to terminate an objective before completion or maturation.

The girl at the counter, the one who adds things up, who takes stock, is none other than Jessica taking a long look, checking herself out, listening to the voice of her own wisdom—she is OK and doesn't need anything. Thus, negating the pregnancy becomes life-affirming, as this realization suggests Jessica's self-acceptance. When Jessica looks back she is examining her past, and it is no surprise that she finds "the girl no longer there," as Jessica is no longer *the girl* but rather a self-reliant *woman* with the independence and wherewithal to make her own decisions and diagnoses, her own evaluations and conclusions, a woman very much in control of her life: mind, body, and spirit. Best of all, she has befriended herself, as she is her own angel.

This next dream is most interesting in that it recounts an abortion, both figurative and literal. The dream was dreamt by **Sheila Ryan:**

> *I was at some celebration but it was unhappy. There were people all around. I went to this above ground pool. There was this fish in the pool made of flesh. Someone had poured salt in the pool and the fish were being poisoned. We tried to flush the water out but the fish died. There was a dog with its paws on the pool edge. I said, "good-by, puppy fish." I was crying.*

Sheila Ryan, the former wife of James Caan, has dreamt an intuitive dream filled with sad recognition. The pool in this dream represents her body with its internal fluids. The water inside the pool seems to be amniotic fluid, as there is a fetus swimming within—a fish made of flesh. The above ground pool is the bulging stomach of the pregnancy. The salt in the pool is reminiscent of the saline-type solution used to induce abortions. To flush something out also refers to an abortion. The abortion is the unhappy event, in that there is a funeral. The puppy symbolizes the baby to whom the dreamer has tearfully said good-bye; the puppy fish is the offspring of the dog. The dog is the father of the baby, and the apathetic onlooker, ''with its paws on the pool edge.''

In another view, the whole dream may be a metaphor for a failed relationship that literally aborted. For, saying good-bye to a life refers to a married lifestyle that went down the tubes, or literally drowned. Here, the salt that was poured into the water may symbolize a preservative, a measure of how the dreamer tried to save her marriage from becoming asphyxiating. Either way, ex-husband Caan, as canine, seems to be in the doghouse.

Mary Shelley had the following dream:

Dreamt that my little baby came to life again; that it had only been cold, and that we rubbed it before the fire, and it lived. Awake and find no baby. (Mary Shelley, Journal, *19 March 1815)*

This is a creative dream that visualizes the product of the writing process in human terms. That which is produced is given life; that which remains unwritten is dead. The baby (the unfinished work) that was thought dead comes to life again, as this is the wish for a creative force, a will to create.

Inspiration needs to be rekindled, as it is perceived as cold. This symbolizes that the creative juices have not been flowing. The dream contains a wishful answer to writer's block. The passions of the heart must be stimulated, the heat of emotions must get fired up.

29

Dreams of Losing a Baby During Pregnancy

D reams of expectant mothers are often filled with anxiety over the well-being of their babies. Therefore, it is not altogether unusual that **Madonna** dreamt the following anxiety dream:

> I went to the doctor and she said, "Oh, the fetal heart-beat is really weak. I want to do an ultra sound," and when she did, she said, "the baby's dead. You have pushed yourself too hard, and the baby's dead." And I watched the baby detach itself from the placenta and sort of float around in my stomach, and I was sobbing hysterically, thinking I killed my baby—My God, I've killed my baby (Vogue, November 1996).

What is interesting, however, is that Madonna remembers dialogue important in understanding the dream's true meaning. It is Madonna as doctor who makes the harsh prognosis that the baby is dead, for the baby *is* Madonna lamenting the lost child of her own youth. It is the sad pronouncement that Madonna is baby no longer, in that mother forever replaces that role. For as we know, motherhood carries the full weight of responsibility on its comforting shoulders; it is a selfless job that requires endless patience. Let's face it, the one who cares, nurtures, and protects can no longer be footloose and fancy-free, but must acquire or at least project a grown-up mentality. This is a demanding task that takes time getting used to since it calls for a change in self-image and behavior and often alters one's lifestyle.

Indeed, Madonna may feel she has pushed herself into this pregnancy prematurely, which seems to have elicited a what-have-I-done attitude. Thus, Madonna hysterically sobs not only for the loss of her childhood, but in self-recrimination, for she has pushed herself too hard.

The image of watching the baby detach itself from the placenta reveals that the baby is not viewed merely as an extension of the parent. The detachment symbol indicates the nonsymbiotic nature of the mother-to-be and reflects that Madonna does not wish to control or manipulate as a parent but will allow her child the freedom and space she needs to develop an independent spirit.

Most important, the dream reveals Madonna's conscientious nature, as she is already attentive, watching her baby with motherly concern.

30

Sexual Dreams With Erotic Fantasies

The following dream is **Samuel Taylor Coleridge**'s famous poem, *Kubla Khan,* which was composed entirely while the poet was sleeping—unconscious in his wondrous world of pleasure domes. The poem was much longer than the fifty lines that remain but unfortunately fate knocked at the door in the guise of a postal delivery man just as Coleridge was writing down all he remembered verbatim. Necessarily, after attending to the business at hand, Coleridge could not recall the rest of the dream, as it had disappeared from his memory. I have reason to believe that many of the remaining lines were lost to repression as the poem is highly sexual in content. The partial poem/dream (edited for the purpose of this analysis) follows:

In Xanadu did Kubla Khan a stately pleasure-dome decree: where . . . the sacred river, ran through caverns measureless to man down to a sunless sea. . . . Fertile ground with walls and towers were girdled round: and there were gardens bright where blossomed many an incense-bearing tree; and here were forests ancient as the hills, enfolding sunny spots of greenery. But oh! That deep romantic chasm which slanted down the green hill. . . . A savage place! . . . was haunted by woman wailing for her demon-lover! And from this chasm, with ceaseless turmoil seething, as if this earth in fast thick pants were breathing, a mighty fountain momentarily forced: . . . and 'mid the dancing rocks at once and ever it flung momentarily the sacred river . . . then reached the caverns measureless to man, and sank in tumult to a lifeless ocean: and mid this tumult Kubla heard from far ancestral voices prophesying war! . . . And all who heard . . . should cry, Beware! Beware! Weave a circle round him thrice, and close your eyes with holy dread, for he on honey-dew hath fed, and drunk the milk of paradise.

Xanadu is the hidden dream world where Coleridge, as Kubla Khan, "decrees" an oxymoronic image: a *"stately pleasure dome."* As stately differs dramatically from associations of pleasure, a more dignified setting is conjured in an attempt to veil the baser oedipal instincts presented in the dream. But the river running through the uncharted "measureless caverns" of the female anatomy neither disguises its sexual content nor its phallic significance as it bears down to the sea. The sea is sunless, as the son has not yet entered the internal, amniotic sea of the mother/womb that Coleridge wishes to return to in oedipal fulfillment.

The fertile ground represents an area to implant seeds and another womb reference, as it is "girdled round" and protected. The "garden bright" symbolizes the female garden from which life blossoms. The forests and hills are ancient, as they relate to the child's anatomical view of the mother's enfolding greenery about to be entered. But there is danger present: the "deep romantic chasm" is a savage place where paternal reprisals are a feared reality. Yet, when the singular woman/mother wails for her demon-lover, Coleridge complies, as her "chasm" needs to be filled. Terming himself demon-lover is Coleridge's way of indulging his oedipal drive with a critical eye. The sexual references of "ceaseless turmoil seething" and "fast thick pants" precede the orgasmic "mighty fountain forced," as the "dancing rocks" of male genitalia, "fling up" the sacred river. Only now is Coleridge threatened by ancestral, fatherly voices "prophesying war," in a castration substitute. Therefore, "all who heard" or found out what occurred "should cry Beware" as Coleridge defensively weaves a magic "circle round him thrice" to be absolutely sure he may ward off punishment from the father. In an oedipal allusion, eyes are closed in "holy dread" in an attempt to repress the forbidden wish fulfillment, for the dreamer, in sexually charged imagery, has fed on the "honey-dew" and has drunk the mother's "milk of Paradise."

31

New-Identity Dreams

New-identity dreams usually represent figures of admiration that the dreamer wishes to bond with in the hopes of experientially understanding the persona behind the history. The following new-identity dream was dreamt by **Jacqueline Kennedy Onassis**. It is a fragment of a daydream/dream recollection as told to Jackie's stepbrother, Hugh D. Auchincloss III in the summer of 1950:

> *We were in a castle, just after walking through the medieval walled town of Carcassonne in Southern France, when I imagined myself a grand heroine like Joan of Arc.*

In reiteration of what has been stated many times previously, homes symbolically refer to the inner walled-in private space that encloses the individual, and they are considered reflections of the personality. Therefore, the more palatial the home, the grander the sense of self. Castles represent the majestic wisdom of an old soul, the remoteness of a personality, and often reveal the wish for a protected and insulated existence. A castle symbolizes a sense of elevation and aloofness—raised above the mainstream of life—and denotes a certain inaccessibility.

The ancient setting of Carcassonne with its medieval walled town may have been the antecedent that inspired Jacqueline with heroic thoughts of defending one's town against invaders. This suggests why Jackie imagined herself like Joan of Arc, who rose with inexorable strength above the mundane fears of mortality and vulnerability. Identifying with a martyr reveals Jackie's romantic nature, her imaginative flair for the dramatic, her adventurous spirit and innate sense of valor. It also reveals a profound gift of prophecy— she later inhabits a symbolic castle, the White House (code-termed Castle in 1963 by the U.S. Secret Service Communications Agency), and becomes the ultimate martyr of the twentieth century. Interestingly, the daydream can also be interpreted as a prelude to the saintly Camelot era of her invention.

The following new-identity dream belongs to the actor, **Abe Vigoda:**

> *I dreamt I was Mahatma Gandhi. I envisioned myself dressed like him in a white robe down to the floor, on the banks of the Ganges where they float dead bodies.*

As Gandhi represents the all-embracing human figure, the wise old man, or guardian, this is a dream about understanding Abe's selfhood. When Abe envisions himself as Mahatma, which literally means great soul, he is looking for new meaning in life. The white robe, a symbol of purity and religious devotion, allows Abe to bond with spiritual truth in his quest to overcome the difficulty of feeling his mortality without fear. Wearing a white robe down to the floor indicates the wish to be in touch with the earth, its vastness and permanence.

Abe is on the banks of the Ganges, bordering on spiritual discovery. When Abe looks down from the sacred banks of the Ganges he finds "dead bodies floating," caught in the flow of existence, as symbolized by the river. This is a wish fulfillment to preside over the passage of time and to accept the rites of renewal, or resurrection, where life is both departing and starting anew—for the Hindus believe that those who die in the Ganges will be carried to paradise. The dead bodies float on the surface rather than sink to the depths, suggesting the dreamer's desire to stay on top of the situation. Perhaps the wish of the dreamer is to cleanse himself in the waters to purify himself from all of Hollywood's rampant cinematic violence. One thing is certain: Becoming Gandhi represents Abe's desire for peace and understanding in his search for truth.

32

Dreams of Not Being Able to Move or Speak

D reams of not being able to move or speak are quite common and usually signify that the dreamer is in conflict. Being in conflict literally means not knowing which way to turn, which is why this type of dream often has the paralyzing effect of creating stasis—as conflict is not usually permissive of aggressive action either in one direction or the other. These dreams speak volumes (albeit sometimes silently) about indecisiveness: the dreamers are usually "sitting on the fence" (or should I say stuck on the fence) betwixt and between.

The following recurrent dream fragment was dreamt by the male supermodel, **Cameron:**

I can never seem to run very fast or run away from things or people. It suddenly all becomes slow motion when I try to run.

Even a simple dream fragment like the one above reflects a complex way of looking at things. As an anxiety dream, and, in a sense, a dream of inhibition, the dream reveals motives for resistance or reluctance on the part of the dreamer. The dream is involved with the conflict between movement and stasis where an unresolved choice can render one motionless. The dreamer may, in fact, seek this powerless condition that forestalls decision making; in simpler terms, the dreamer may not be able to (or not know how to) say no. Restrictions are placed by individuals on themselves as a measure of precaution, or for the purpose of self-punishment. The dreamer wants to run but is being thwarted by his own body, by the unwillingness of his own legs to move effortlessly. (Some dreamers have reported feeling the heaviness and futility of trying to move quickly through waist-high water.) Thus, as the decision to move is not operational, the dream reveals the classic fear of loss of control. This may suggest that the dreamer feels that he is not controlling his life decisions or that the decisions he has made are not being followed through to fruition.

Additionally, not running fast enough signifies that there is not enough time. Perhaps demands are being made that the dreamer is unprepared to accede to. In actuality, the desire may be to flee, but out of an innate sense of obligation and responsibility, the dreamer is unable to do so. He instead becomes motionless or moves slowly, as if he is in slow motion. Yet this movement that is perceived as being in slow motion is at the specific request of the dreamer; in other words, the dreamer wishes to have more time to evaluate the situation at hand, almost in freeze-frame. The dreamer needs to assimilate all the details and weigh the options available to him—this reflects the thoughtful, conscientious and nonimpulsive nature of the dreamer. Interestingly, the dreamer desires to keep at bay not only people but things that he cannot run away from. These things may be interpreted as situations or decisions. The lack or difficulty of moving often reflects a desire to tread softly in life, not to violate, trespass, or evoke anger.

Another dream where movement was restricted is one wherein the dreamer was trying hard to move forward even though someone was calling his name from behind. He did not look back, but as hard as he tried to progress, he simply could not move ahead and was forced to remain stationary for the remainder of the dream, as though his body had turned into the trunk of a tree.

In actuality, the dreamer did not really want to proceed in the direction his current life was headed, as he had just gotten separated from his wife and was contemplating getting a swift divorce. However, he had evidentially placed behind him the very situation that had made him anxious (hence, he does not look behind him in the dream). The couple had not gone for any marital counseling, but by discussing his dream, the dreamer was able to realize that he was unable to decide the correct course of action—he felt that he may have been rushing into something that he would later regret. With this in mind it is no wonder that his dream wish was not to move, but to slow down a rapidly moving process. Thus, the dream was a successful attempt at slowing down the momentum, of being carried away by the impulsive wings of emotion.

33

Dreams of Responsibility

Responsibility dreams are dreams wherein the dreamer comes to a realization that forces a life change or alters his or her way of thinking. An example of such a dream would be one that depicts the evils of smoking to the extent that upon awakening the dreamer chucks the Camels or whatever brand he or she was inhaling into the nearest waste bin. These are dreams of conscience—and dreams in which a decision is made as a result of that conscience. These are dreams of reflection and attitude change. The following is a responsibility dream that was dreamt by the singer/composer **John Waite:**

It's dawn. England. A country road. I'm in a green Morgan sports car. It's Spring. I'm bouncing down the road in sharp focus, taking the corners at 120 mph like the car is driving itself. To my right, there's a girl in my car. She's Scottish, wearing tartan plaid. I know this girl from another life. She come to find me in this dream. Happy, I pull the car over and we start to make love. It's fantastic. After a while I feel someone is following me. I'm being chased. We get back on the road heading for his factory from W.W.II hoping to lose them on side roads. This is my home town. I walk up a side road into this building. Crates of cattle are being butchered alive. They're looking at me with this pleading expression. I think to myself, I'll never eat meat again. (After the dream I became a vegetarian.)

Symbols of dawn and Spring indicate that a rebirth or resurrection of spirit is about to occur. Thus, John is in sharp focus, as he is at a turning point, taking corners at blinding speed. The car driving itself represents the motors of history that are beyond individual control. The girl symbolizes enlightenment, serving as John's moral guide, as the blissful beginning of the dream is darkly contrasted with the dream's second half wherein the dreamer detours off the country road in favor of the road less traveled and faces the grim reality of the world's cruelty—inside a factory from World War II, "crates of cattle are being slaughtered alive." (Interestingly, the dream has the girl *mistakenly* seated on the side of the right, which symbolizes the dream's righteous tone; as all British steering wheels are on the right, the girl would necessarily have to sit on the left side of the front seat.)

The cattle which are humanized by their pleading expression, become a metaphor for Holocaust victims, victims of war, and, in general, the plight of all human suffering. John's conscious sensitivity, awareness, and abhorrence of the horrors perpetrated by humankind have given him the unconscious realization (within his dream) that one can only make one's own small moral acts, such as deciding to become a vegetarian, "never to eat meat again." The dream shows that John's unconscious was one step ahead of his conscious mind in that the dream is the event that motivates the action. As of this writing John Waite is still a vegetarian!

The following dream of responsibility was dreamt by
Judge Philip Maier:

I am in bed with some woman and we are lying there
naked, and all of a sudden there are these attorneys
that are arguing a legal point to me. I have to make a
ruling on it. I'm trying to get up and the woman starts
snoring and I'm feeling a little embarrassed because it
is not really appropriate to be in bed with a woman
while you're trying to make a decision. I'm trying to
get up and she's holding onto me. I get up and listen to
the arguments. Then I awaken.

This is a dream of moral and ethical conscience wherein
the obligation to remain impartial is sought after. The nakedness symbolizes the vulnerability of the judge to succumb to
judgmental bias. The woman represents the naked truth,
which is stripped of its emotional content. As the woman
snores she necessarily has her eyes closed, which seems a
symbolic reminder that justice is blind.

In noting that "it is not really appropriate to be in bed
with a woman while you're trying to make a decision" the
point is made that emotions should never enter into the logis-
tics of the decision-making process. Similarly, the dreamer
reveals that he will not be "in bed" with any side of an argu-
ment or case, for he wants his decision to be objective and
bias free.

The dreamer is entirely aware that the heart is capable of
being subverted or pulled down as evidenced by the woman
holding onto the dreamer, who is trying to get up and listen to
the legalities of the decisions. The dreamer is seen to symbolically embrace both the spirit and the letter of the law.

34

Divorce Dreams

Most divorce dreams depict the house in shambles, with much work to be done, wherein the female dreamer is running around making alterations and repairs, and re-decorating. As mentioned throughout this text, a symbol of a house represents the being or sense of self of the dreamer, a divorce symbolizes a divided house or a house in upheaval.

Divorces usually leave the dreamer feeling emotionally drained or detached, with feelings of remorse, guilt, failure, and lack of stability. The self-image, usually fragmented and in need of repair, often manifests itself in a badly run-down house, or a house that needs reconstruction or redecoration. The following divorce dream was dreamt by **Mai Hallingby:**

> *I'm in a house with people in New York. At a party. I don't know whether people are coming or going. But outside there was another house being built that was incomplete. A house I was trying to finish. There was fog outside—mist, so I didn't quite see who was out there.*

As a house symbolizes who we are and the lifestyle we lead, being at a party where people are coming and going represents Mai caught up in the frenetic social whirl of society. The first house is the social posturing of the external per-

sona. The other house being built *outside* in the dream's way
of disguise—for this is the *internal* private realm where outside indicates separate. This is the part of Mai that needs
more space; it suggests that something is under construction—in the works—that this is a period of personal growth.
(Mai is involved in a divorce.)

The house is incomplete, as it is an ongoing creation. (It is
currently without a husband.) There is underlying structure
but it must be built upon, dealt with. Because things are a bit
foggy, Mai doesn't have all the answers; the fog softens
things and blurs the sharp edges of existence that snag us
every now and then. But "trying to finish" the house shows
determination and is self-affirming. The dream imagery
shows, however, that Mai is on the verge of self-discovery
and self-acceptance of her new autonomy. Not seeing the
whole picture, she cannot quite see who is out there, but she's
close—because the fog lifts! (Perhaps Mr. Right is just
around the corner.)

The following dream was dreamt by **Laura Hunt:**

*I was driving in my car and there was this large peli-
can flying that crashed into the front of my car. I
looked at his face and was shocked to see the sweet
face of an old man. I was sobbing uncontrollably. I felt
overwhelmed by sorrow.*

The driver of a car is the one in charge of the situation—
the responsible one, as the wheel of life is symbolically in her
hands. (This may signify that Laura is blaming herself for her
divorce.) A head-on collision represents a meeting of the
ways—the wish for connection. Crashing into someone is
confrontational and means that there is a desire to make an

impact, but it may also reflect the wish to make someone who is inaccessible accessible, to make someone halt, to gain someone's attention.

The large pelican represents a scavenger who will hunt, but it also conceals an obscure reference to the surname of Laura's ex. The bird symbolizes a lofty, free-spirited individual (of course, the bird may symbolize other past relationships in addition to Laura's ex, as birds of a feather flock together, but the symbol does not change—it still bemoans a break-up), for the bird has risen above the daily restraints of existence. There was distance between the driver and the pelican that made the relationship falter. Thus, the dream is a crash course in communication that reestablishes contact—for there were words left unspoken. There is sorrowful misperception—the dreamer is shocked to see the "sweet face of an old man" on a pelican's body. But recognition is reached when Laura perceives sweetness and even helplessness in someone previously perceived as being aloof and independent. The dream expresses great sorrow and mortification.

The following dream was dreamt by **Anthony Quinn** while he was still in the midst of his divorce proceedings. The dream reveals that Anthony had mixed feelings and some regrets about his divorce action:

I live on the edge of a placid lake. The house is not big enough. Behind me is a big stone ruined castle. I am trying to buy it. But as I walk through it I realize is not practical for modern living as all rooms are off a long, long passage. But I am not happy living in the house while the ruined castle is behind me. I love the view from that castle. I walk through both houses never at rest.

As legends often occur in medieval settings, the legendary Anthony Quinn has aptly dreamt of himself in a castle. And there is drama, too. Whereas a placid lake symbolizes reflection and gives man a surface view of himself, being on the edge of this lake suggests that the dreamer is ready to take the plunge—to find what is concealed beneath the depths of consciousness: this indicates Mr. Quinn is on the verge of self-discovery. A house not big enough indicates a stifled, restrictive, or claustrophobic sense of being (Anthony needs room to roam), as homes represent the dreamer's state of mind. But in dreams spatial relations also refer to time, and, as such, the big stone castle affords the eternal and unalterable sense of permanence—Anthony's ties to his estranged wife. The "stone ruined" castle is a fortification that has withstood the wrath of time.

In that the castle is placed behind the dreamer, it symbolizes the landscape of the past; the castle beckons with its memories and the dreamer loves the view. But recapturing the past is neither feasible, nor accessible, as "all rooms are off a long, long passage" of time that can no longer be accessed. The dreamer desires the cool remoteness and introspection that the castle affords but cannot deny himself the practicalities of modern living. "Walking through two houses," the dreamer perceives two worlds, the world of the conscious and of the unconscious, the different relationships of past and present, a division within himself. And like the ghost in *Hamlet* the dreamer walks through the world of the dead (the past) and of the living (the present) never at rest, a great kingly spirit seeking an emotional resolution, or self-justification in his life situation.

35

Dreams of
Dying

Dreams wherein the dreamers perceive themselves to be
dead are often dreamt as a form of self-sacrifice by
dreamers who are anticipating leaving the home for an
extended period of time or are planning to abandon something in their lives, such as a career, a familial or romantic
relationship, or a creed. This predetermined abandonment
necessitates the feeling of guilt, whereby the dream doles out
its punishment in the killing off of the dreamer.

But there is another meaning to this seemingly morbid
nocturnal scenario. The death may be a guiltless one—symbolic of the dreamer embarking on a new life. The death is
the death of the old self, the old existence. The dream serves
as a validation of a change in lifestyle and makes available a
visual manifestation of closure. The following example of a
funeral dream was dreamt by an editor friend of mine; it is a
recurring dream wherein the mourners change (with the exception of the dreamer's parents who are always present) in
relation to whomever is in the dreamer's life at the moment
of the dream:

I dream I am at my own funeral at my childhood
church. The coffin is already at the front of the church,
and all my relatives are there grieving. I do not see

myself. I am a presence, sort of hovering above. A mu-
sician (a former boyfriend) is playing ''Every Grain of
Sand.''

This dream occurred just before the dreamer was about to
leave for an extended stay in Italy, wherein her departure was
symbolized as a kind of death. Feelings of guilt are represented through grieving relatives. The childhood church is
significant because the dreamer's departure is literally seen
as a departure from childhood to adulthood—the dreamer is
leaving the roost. The relatives are there to validate the experience. But the dream is one of decisiveness, as the coffin is
already at the front of the church—meaning that the case is
closed. Whereas the dream represents finality it also signifies
new beginnings. The funeral is for the death of the old self
(particularly the death of the dependent child), which engenders the birth of the dreamer's independent spirit, which is
''a presence, hovering above,'' without any wistfulness or
longing.

Indicating that a transformation has been made, the
dreamer does not see herself. Yet, the dream is self-
referential, as it has a conscience. There is the recognition of
the finality of endings as represented by the (former boyfriend) musician, who plays ''Every Grain of Sand.'' The
-hourglass symbolism of the song signifies the passage of
time and encourages reflections about personal insignifi-
cance—a consolation of sorts—for in the long run, time nullifies all actions and choices.

36

Dreams of
Aliens

Believe it or not, dreaming of aliens is fairly common as aliens often symbolize the deceased—those who have passed to the other side. The deceased are viewed as something alien, as they can no longer be communicated with or seen. Their lifestyle can no longer be assessed in human terms, as they are believed to have superior or supernatural powers—invisibility, the ability to go through walls, etc. The main point is that they can no longer be understood and thus are symbolic of something alien.

Dreaming of aliens may also symbolize the dreamer's own sense of alienation from society—the sense of being disconnected or cut off from the world. The following childhood dream was dreamt by a friend:

I was abducted by aliens. They were little men (my height) who were all wearing yellow fisherman raincoats with metal attachments. We were standing eye to eye. They took me for a long ride in a yellow taxi cab— a Checker cab (just like the one my father had driven at night during much of my childhood years). The taxi was waiting up a steep hill. They put a rubber band around my wrist which meant that I was connected to them and that I would be able to understand them

> *while in their presence. Then we went to the rooftop of*
> *a tall building and they quizzed me, and examined me.*
> *They did not speak but were communicating to me by*
> *mental telepathy or thoughts. I was able to receive this*
> *communication because of the rubber band. After-*
> *wards, I was brought back home. Because of my cour-*
> *teous manner I felt that I accomplished something; that*
> *I had saved the world.*

In this dream the dreamer conveys her own childhood feelings of being alienated from her father, and reveals her wish to establish a paternal closeness. The yellow taxi symbolizes the dreamer's father in that this was his profession during many of her childhood years. The taxi that is waiting up a steep hill represents the father's inaccessibility. Riding in the taxi reveals the dreamer's desire to spend time with her father in close quarters. The aliens do not speak aloud but rather communicate through telepathy, which both replicates the laconic personality of the dreamer's father and establishes the wish of the dreamer to learn a way to communicate with her father—a way to understand what her father is thinking. It is also the wish to have a deep, profound communication that is "beyond words." The dreamer is quizzed and examined, which is a reversal of her desire to quiz her father. The Checker Cab, although the actual type taxi the father had driven, is symbolized herein because it fits in nicely with the motive of the dream—it reinforces the image of checking something out in order to make sense of it.

Being eye to eye with the aliens is yet another attempt to see eye to eye, to be of the same mind. The father is enlarged into more than one figure as a means of disguised recognition (for after all, the bold wish of the dream is for the daughter to abduct the father). It is not uncommon that a father's presence is viewed as being larger than life. The rubber band is a symbol of what holds something together—the desired bond between daughter and father. The metal attachments on the raincoats symbolize the wish for an emotional attachment, as the parental attachment is now cold as metal.

Being taken to the rooftop of a tall building symbolizes the brain—the mental processes, for the motive of this dream is to understand, to assess the puzzling, distant presence of the father. The dream ends with the dreamer thinking that she has accomplished something, or saved the world. As the world represents the father, the dreamer wishes to be commended for her "courteous" behavior, her act of courting her father in the hopes of staving off a detached relationship.

Another example of an alien dream was dreamt by a doctoral student who had just lost her husband:

This is a two-part dream: In the first part, I was with a man who was an alien from another planet; in the second, I had become that alien. Dream 1—He looked just like a man—tall stocky, grey/white hair, clean-shaven. And he spoke remarkably good English. But the first part of the dream centered on trying to get a de-coding book or system, because he wanted to communicate or speak in his own language. We were in a library. I worked for some government agency. I was trying to get a "security clearance" for him, to get access to coding material. There were 5 or 6 long pencils— stone-grey or brown—prism-shaped. I explained to one of the secretaries/reference librarians that the man used these to write up and down, a bit like Chinese.

The bureaucrats were difficult and frustrating about the "security clearance."

Dream 2—In the second part of the dream I was the man, and I was unbearably lonely. The woman (my other self?) had gone to New York, and I was left alone, in San Francisco. I wanted to be with her, because even though she didn't understand, she was much closer to understanding than most people. Her daughter (looked like Gabriella) was wearing my favorite dress, but it was lower-cut than mine, and with lace covering the bodice. She was going to NY to meet her mother. I tried to go too, but "they" wouldn't stop or see me running to go with them. I apologized to a general I ran into, for not seeing him, but I explained that I was very caught up in looking for "her" and could see no one else. All the while I was so tired, I kept looking for somewhere to lie down, and also desperately lonely. I remember thinking that phrase from the New Testament, "the birds of the air have nests, and the foxes have dens, but the Son of Man has nowhere to lay his head," and feeling that I needed to lay my head in someone's lap. I had no companion, and a sense of being alien and different. Terrible isolation with no end.

The first part of the dream summons up the remembrance of the dreamer's deceased husband in the disguise of a man who is identified as being an alien from another planet. The planet symbolizes the world of the beyond. The decoding book represents the wish to commune with the dead, who are represented as having their own language. The dream is one of longing where the dreamer is desperately trying to find a system to cope with her feelings of loneliness and despair. The dream is not just a wish for communication with the dead but the wish to gain information, to be informed of the kind of language her departed husband is fluent in.

Trying to gain security clearance for the alien symbolizes that the dreamer wants her husband to be allowed to pass through—to come back to earth, to the world of the living. Her mission is to get access to coding material to decipher the world beyond.

The dreamer looks toward governmental intervention, as the government is viewed as a parental figure, an agency of information that knows all the rules and regulations. On one level, the pencils that write up and down in vertical fashion symbolize a message from up above (heaven) to down below (earth), but encoded in the word "pencils" is the word "penis," the pencils with their up and down movement represent the dreamer's wish for physical contact—to have sex with her deceased husband. Thus, gaining clearance is a metaphor that means she wants him to be able to enter in the sexual sense of the word.

In the second part of the dream, by assuming the role of the man (or husband), the dreamer is not recognized (by herself), which reinforces her lack of recognition and loss of identity—she is "caught up in looking" for herself—for who she has become since the death of her husband. But the fact that the dreamer goes unrecognized is a consolation that allows the dreamer to imagine that perhaps her deceased husband is around her but in an unrecognizable form, so that she is unable to see him.

The phrase from the New Testament reveals the dreamer's sense of being homeless, with no place to "lay her head," as the home represents who we are; for without her husband the dreamer no longer knows her place in society, or where she will fit in. The dream reveals the need to be comforted. Her grief has made her feel different—so much so that she envisions herself as an alien breed, cut off from society, in emotional isolation.

Most important, by becoming her deceased husband, the dreamer is able to assure herself that she is longed for and missed, and to be consoled that her husband is mourning her absence as much as she is his, *that theirs is a shared loneliness*—as this loneliness is perceived as being a continuous bond between the dreamer and her deceased husband.

The following alien dream was dreamt by **Alexandros:**

> *I am driving in my jeep with my mother in a square tunnel of ice. It is night. There is a wall of ice in front of me—it's the end of the road. I stop and look out and up from my window. I see snow everywhere. I cannot go anywhere else. There is a forest of trees in the distance. Above the wall of ice, hovering in the air there are two "light beings" and a vehicle in the middle that is oval shaped like an egg, but sideways. On either side of the vehicle is a "light being" around four feet tall; they are shaped out of light with not many features. They are looking at me and smiling. I say to my mother, "Look at those beings looking at us," but my mother could not see anyone.*

Driving in a square tunnel of ice that leads to a dead end symbolizes that the dreamer is blocked—there is a claustrophobic sense of being buried alive. Movement has halted and there is no longer any advancement or progression forward as the dreamer finds himself up against a wall, and at the end of the road. This means that the only way out is up. Up signifies the wish to rise above one's problematic existence, to transcend to a higher level of consciousness.

At this stasis the dreamer must make a change in his life. This is the wished-for transformation from the material world of density (as represented by the water that has transformed into ice and snow) to the ethereal world of immaterial light. Ice, as a symbol, often signifies the reverse of an erection as it becomes hard in the cold, unlike the phallus that hardens from the heat of excitation. Thus, the ice herein reveals the dreamer's alienation or disconnection from the barren landscape of the mundane world he wishes to raise himself beyond. The distant forest of trees is the fertile ground the dreamer aspires to.

The dream includes many references to sight: looking and seeing is emphasized. The dream makes usage of the phonetic rendering of the word "ice" which symbolizes eyes. The dreamer is confronted by a wall of eyes, which is the maternal watchfulness incorporated into the societal realm. What is clear is that the dreamer wishes to transcend beyond sight and public scrutinization, which is perceived as a blight on creativity, to reenter the "egg-shaped vehicle"—the womb of creativity.

The dreamer is symbolized by his vehicle: a jeep—a land car that is grounded, bound by the earth. The "light beings" or spirit guides represent the rescuers—the ones that bring life. They are the harbingers of the new "egg-shaped" vehicle, which symbolizes the chance of fertilization in an otherwise sterile environment. The wish of the dreamer is to trade vehicles, to become a lighter soul. He wishes this enlightenment for his mother as well, which is why there are two "light beings" present. But the dreamer's mother cannot see them because she does not see what her son sees—because she thinks and views things differently, which is why she does not see the light.

37

Chess Dreams

The following Chess Dream was dreamt by Mr. K. an avid chess player and a member of the U.S. Chess Federation:

I was somewhat anxious while I was playing the moves, knowing that you have to sacrifice a piece in order to make a gain for strategic reasons: Bishop takes Knight—Bishop takes Bishop—and then the Queen takes D4 and I gain the advantage.

During the day the dreamer had been studying tactical maneuvers to such an extent that these studies in chess became translated into night moves; in his dream he engages in play with an imaginary adversary. He is concerned with contemplating moves—the strategy of living. For the game of chess is a microcosm of the game of life where sometimes one has to take a backward step in order to move two steps ahead. The dream deals with the philosophic concepts of sacrifice and survival—and warns against letting down one's guard.

On a simplistic level the dream is one of self-affirmation wherein the dreamer is viewed as the winner, the master of tactics and strategies—because he is one step ahead of the rest. Yet, a deeper level of meaning reveals that the disguised wish of the dream is to cleverly gain advantage over the king or father figure (through eventual checkmate), which in oedipal fashion will permit the dreamer to gain possession of the king's queen, the mother. (It must be noted that the last name of the dreamer's father begins with the letter K.) Thus, the oedipal threat of castration is couched within the knowledge that a ''piece must be sacrificed to make a gain.'' The sacrificial piece is, of course, the phallus.

38

Identity Dreams

Identity dreams are dreams wherein the dreamer is seeking deeper self-knowledge. These dreams often occur before or after major life changes: marriages, divorces, deaths, new occupations, or a geographical relocation. The following dream was dreamt by a literary agent and attorney during the process of her divorce:

> *I was looking for a business card, and going from place to place looking at the different types of cards, the different colors. At first I kept looking at the traditional color ecru background with lots of small black lettering. The card would appear to me in my mind with lots of information on the card. Then I saw this card and I just started smiling. This was my card! It was my favorite color blue, a blue sky with white clouds and my name in the middle in white.*

Looking for a business card that expresses the personality behind the card is symbolic enough as cards are paper thin and pressed flat—the emotions of one going through the process of a divorce. The card as carrier of information symbolizes the need for self-recognition, identity, and self-worth—

senses of self that dog-ear at the edges during stressful periods in one's life.

Looking for the right card is crucial as the card represents
a personal statement about strength, about using your trump
card; honesty, about having your cards on the table; hidden
agenda, about having an ace up your sleeve; savvy, about
playing your cards right; and sanity, as in not playing with a
full deck.

Looking at the background with the small black lettering
is a direct reference to the divorce proceedings—the dreamer
must remain aware of the fine print.

Not choosing a traditional card means the dreamer is per-
mitting herself greater freedom of expression and creativity.
When the dreamer finally finds her card, she is overjoyed; it
is sky blue with white clouds; her name is "in the middle in
white." Thus, she "divines" herself by putting her name up
in the sky. She has risen in a flight of self-affirmation. The
color white symbolizes purity and enlightenment—starting
anew with a clean slate, a paper version of a tabula rasa.

The following recurring identity dream was dreamt by a
brilliant young research scientist when he was only seven
years old. What is incredible about this dream is that it
clearly shows the direction that the dreamer's life will take,
which is proof that the dreamer was already aware of his life
choice and his desire to help mankind. Moreover, the dream
may be viewed as a prophetic and inspirational tool in that
even in low moments it serves as a constant source of inspiration to the dreamer:

> *I see myself in the universe. There is no gravity and I
> am floating around in a sort of liquid environment (like
> what I experience underwater when I am scuba-*

diving). There are flashes of light. There are huge bub-
bles which I realize are cells. I am riding on one of the
cells as though the cell is a chariot. There was a war
going on between the good cells and the bad cells. I am
on a good cell fighting a bad cell. There are different
colors around me. At first the colors are relatively dark
but then they change to lighter colors. Then, in bright
light, I find something to destroy the bad cells. Now
there is pure white light and I know that I have suc-
ceeded.

Seeing oneself in the universe immediately presents a larger view, as this is beyond the material world. Not having to deal with gravity suggests that nothing can weigh down the aspirations of the dreamer, and reflects his independent thinking in that he is going against the grain—he will not be restricted by boundaries or rules.

The flashes of light symbolize inspirational thoughts. The bubbles, which visually appear encased in a membrane, are creatively realized as cells. Whereas the cells phonetically render the symbolization of being imprisoned, riding a cell as if it were a chariot reveals the mastery of the dreamer, external to the cell—giving directions, with the reins in his hand.

The war that is going on between the good and bad cells is a reference to sickness and health—ease and dis-ease. The dreamer, in fighting off the bad cells, is clearly identifying himself as a doctor or research scientist who is working for the benefit of humankind. The dark colors suggest sickness or death and the light colors suggest well-being and life—this is remarkably consistent with current new age views that espouse the curative nature of white light. (Imaging or visualizing white light entering the body is believed to have a curative effect.)

In what may have been a premonitory vision, in bright light, or in the brilliance of the mind, the dreamer makes a discovery—he finds something that destroys the bad cells. Thus, he has succeeded in serving humankind.

In another view the dream can be seen as a wish fulfillment, as the dreamer was himself a sickly child and thus desirous of good health. Imagining that the good cells win represents an optimistic view, a constructive reasoning that will lead to the empowerment of the dreamer. He succeeds in his mission and is self-empowered by the dream to pursue a career in molecular research. (The dreamer is currently working on finding out why the lens of the eye is the only part of the body that is not susceptible to cancer.)

39

Religious Dreams

Religious dreams are dreams that contain religious symbolism, such as icons or visitations of Jesus, the Virgin Mary, or any of the saints or angels. They are dreams that fill dreamers with the sense of hope and of purpose. Often these dreams occur during lows in life situations. They are inspirational and spiritual in nature. They foster thoughts beyond the mundane world of the material. The following religious dream was dreamt by **Helen Sanders,** a radio show producer, while she was in between jobs:

I was back in the home I grew up in (in reality, the house had burned to the ground years before). In the living room next to the upright piano I had played and practiced on in youth, in the corner was a statuette sized Mother Mary. She threw spheres rotating in mid-air to my two brothers and me. I received two, one I understood was for my mother whom I have taken care of and looked after most of my life because of her four mental breakdowns—the other sphere was for me. My brothers did not walk but floated ahead of me on their journey with their spheres. I felt I was being lead [sic] through my journey by the spirit of Mary, but that part of my burden would be carrying the sphere (the ball) for my mother. I was being shown that everything in my physical world was not solid as it appeared to be— and that it was a substance that barely existed—a substance that was penetrable. For some reason, though, when I reached the kitchen area, there was a lead surface that I could not pierce through. I did not know why at the time of the dream.

Months after this dream Helen lost two rooms of storage that included her piano and other treasured possessions— handmade furniture that was made by her father, and numerous irreplaceable childhood photographs. Although devastated by her loss, Helen managed to recollect her strange and mystical dream, which she interpreted as being a forewarning of how to deal with the fire that was to come. She viewed the dream as a lesson about the meaning of life and the necessity of letting go of material things as they were shown to be transitory or immaterial. But definitely not *solid.*

The statuette of "Mother Mary" symbolizes the wish to be nurtured and cared for. The statuette that "threw rotating spheres" or balls to the dreamer symbolically reveals that the weight of the world is in the dreamer's hands, as the dreamer is the one who is responsible for her mother. In a paranormal sense (in that seraphim have been described as being able to rotate themselves into spheres or discs), the angels are leading the dreamer on a journey toward a specific wisdom. The rotation of the spheres symbolizes the circularity of time, which signifies that life is not without its highs and lows. In other words, what goes around comes around. The subliminal message behind the rotation of the spheres is meant to enlighten the dreamer, which is why she floats. The knowledge that nothing is solid will be useful later on when the dreamer loses many possessions in a fire.

In no uncertain terms this was a period of instability for the dreamer which the dream symbolizes by the physical world appearing as a nonsolid, nonpermanent, unstable substance. This may symbolize the mental state of the dreamer's mother, as the mother had had four mental breakdowns. As the house represents who we are, going through the house represents an effort to come to terms with and understand one's persona. The unpenetratable lead surface in the kitchen area represents the mind, (as the kitchen is associated with food, eating and one's mouth—the kitchen symbolically represents the uppermost region of the body). This suggests that within the context of the dream the dreamer was trying but was unable to penetrate the dream's meaning.

Advertising copywriter, **Carol Lupo,** had the following dream of religious awakening. The dream contains a poignant message:

> *I meet Jesus on the road (to where, I do not know, but it's in a warm climate). He is wrapped in white, as Jesus frequently is, but his chest is bare. I greet him with a caress, running my hands over his chest, and I attempt to kiss him. I touch his hair, but he gently pushes me away and says, "You must learn how to love me." I tell him I understand.*

The symbol of being on a road reveals that the dreamer is on a quest for personal discovery. This particular road exists in a warm climate, a warm, loving environment. Jesus or the good is partially wrapped or under wraps, which signifies that he (or goodness) is only partially understood, only partially seen. His chest is bare in that he is baring his heart, his soul. The chest is also a metaphor for a bureau that has draws where possessions are stored. The chest is bare because Jesus is not concerned or weighed down by material things, in that he is enlightened.

The dreamer, still in the realm of the physical, is caught up with and after physical sensations and/or gratifications. The running of the hands over the chest symbolizes the importance of touch—for the dreamer is looking for *sensual* proof that Jesus is real. But in that the dreamer is searching for answers, instruction follows from Jesus, the teacher, the paternal figure. His message is that in going for the physical realm one is inevitably pushed away or removed from the metaphysical or immaterial realm.

By the dream's end the unconsciousness of the dreamer has already transcended the senses such that love (the warm climate) is intuited and no longer based on things material that can be seen or felt. The dreamer that had at first attempted to define love by personifying and embodying its essence has become initiated into an understanding of the platonic ideal.

The following dream was dreamt in 1987 by Lorraine on the morning that a ''harmonic convergence'' was to occur at 7:30 A.M.—when people from all over the world were going to pray for positivity:

> *A light being came to me all of light. He told me he was from Sirius. His name was Lhasa—he was my guide. He showed me how he put white light into people. I saw him take spider webs out of people. He would roll them into a ball and throw them out in a lake. He showed me how when people pray white light emits from their bod-*

ies and spirals around the earth. Then he showed me a
vision of people holding hands all across the earth at
the edge of a cliff. He said that they wouldn't go over if
they were all together in peace.

A dreamer's hopeful thoughts about the effect that the harmonic convergence will have on society have filtered into her dream. The dream's optimistic core envisions a harmonious populace connected to each other by the holding of hands, communal prayer, and trust. If the human daisy chain is broken—if one lets go of a hand—the threat is that all would fall off the cliff. Therefore, whereas letting go is negatively represented, holding on is praised, as it pertains to one's faith and one's personal ideals.

The light being that comes from Sirius symbolizes that this is a serious dream about world peace, as the name Lhasa, is synonymous with and symbolic of the Tibetan city of peace. The spiderwebs represent that which is found in old, dusty places that have not been cared for or visited in a long time: the empty places within the caring part of the heart that people have vacated. Taking these spiderwebs out of people signifies that these soulful places within humans that have fallen into disuse must be gotten into for they have been ignored within the self. The spiderweb also symbolizes the need for entrapment within us all. The altruistic wish expressed in the dream is for people to clean up their act and their consciousness, to work on themselves, for the dreamer envisions each person as a part of the earth and therefore responsible for emitting their own white light.

The symbol of the spiderweb is opposite to the symbol of the lake, as the spiderweb grows unnoticed or unseen whereas the lake represents reflection. Thus, the veil of ignorance is drowned in reflectivity. The spiderweb, as something hidden, is also a metaphor for denial, or what we hide inside ourselves.

The communal holding of hands represents the dreamer's desire to stay connected, and thereby stay in touch with the human condition, which underscores the humanitarian spirit of the dreamer.

40

Discovery
Dreams

D iscovery dreams are similar to problem-solving dreams
and could be considered problem-solvers but whereas
the latter involve settling situations, or making decisions, or correcting faulty ideas or beliefs, discovery dreams
actually make discoveries—some scientific, some philosophic, some practical. The chemist Dmitry Mendeleyev,
who was attempting to develop a system for classifying the
chemical elements according to their atomic weights (which
would enable him to predict the discovery of some unknown
elements), claims to have dreamt of such a system—what we
now call the periodic table.

Descartes supposedly realized that science and philosophy should be linked, after a dream he had wherein he discovered a dictionary and an anthology of poetry that he read.
He interpreted the dream to mean that observational scientific reasoning should be applied to philosophic inquiries.

Elias Howe, the inventor of the sewing machine, discovered the correct placement of the hole at the end of the sewing needle, which then made his whole invention
operational. His dream follows:

*I was captured by a tribe of savages. The king roared,
"Elias Howe, I command you on pain of death to finish*

this machine at once." The tribal lord ordered his warriors to execute me. Then I noticed that at the pointed end of each warrior's spear was an eye-shaped hole.

The tribe of savages symbolizes the metaphorical uninhibited inhabitants of the id who fulfill their every instinct and drive—for the "land of the id" is where the creative and inspirational energies never sleep. This part of the dream would have the potential of spurring Elias on to thoughts of great clarity and significance. The king represents the father figure, the paternal reprimand and demand all in one. The threat of being executed is actually a wish fulfillment that contains the fervent desire to be able to execute a workable needle for his machine. The end of each spear could be interpreted as meaning that Elias Howe was literally at the end of his tether. The spear is the spearhead idea, and the male phallus is the driving force in an action or an endeavor. The eye-shaped hole represents vision or sight. The hole at the end of the spear is the orifice of the phallus from which the seeds of life spill forth—this is the wish for creative inspiration. Thus, the wish expressed in the dream is to bring to fruition Howe's invention or creation.

Coincidentally, this wish was symbolized by the exact image that Elias Howe needed to see. More than anything else the dream reveals how the unconscious mind works while we are sleeping—how involved it remains in the solving of our daily problems.

41

Dreams of Invisibility

Dreams of invisibility are similar to flying dreams where the dreamer is gifted with a powerful and magical skill. Both of the previous dreams fall into the larger category of wish-fulfillment dreams with some elements of self-affirmation thrown in. In that both dreams defy the laws of nature—in terms of what we know as being humanly possible—they indicate the independent spirit of the dreamers. But whereas flying dreams focus on lightening up the dreamer to the point of weightlessness, dreams of invisibility nullify the dreamer's physical existence or presence. Therefore, the purpose of dreaming one is invisible (other than being able to place, under the croupier's nose, the ball in the numbered compartment of your choice and thereby win at roulette) is mostly for matters of protection—to become inconspicuous, to escape notice. These dreams also put an end to expectations or performance anxiety, as the wish is to be on the sidelines away from public scrutiny. Also associated with the act of invisibility is the wish to forget or to be forgotten—as in out of sight, out of mind. The following dream was dreamt by the composer **Alexandros:**

I am with other people—not in dense form—floating in space. Nothing is dense or solid as in real life. I am

*floating. I feel I am being chased by evil dark entities—
demons. We are two sides—the light and the dark beings. I fear. I run as if I am flying. All of a sudden I see
winged see-through entities flying towards us with a
crystal tube the size of an index finger. They touch me
on my left wrist on the veins. I become invisible. I get
connected with the good energy—connected by an umbilical cord made out of light energy. We couldn't be
seen anymore and I felt protected from the bad entities.
I felt secure.*

The statement ''we are two sides'' symbolizes the realization of the dreamer that there is both good and bad in humanity, which is why the dreamer struggles against the dark
beings or forces of existence chasing him. Being chased, in
the phonetic rendering of the word, means that the dreamer
intends to keep his moral and ethical sensibilities intact. But
as the pursuing demons are ''not in dense form,'' they are
difficult to strike down. The dream reveals a dangerous
world; therefore, the wish of the dream is to become connected to the good energy of the celestial mother via an umbilical cord of light. Once connected the dreamer is no longer
able to be seen. This signifies that having sought out the security of the maternal womb, the dreamer has entered the
heavenly womb of the cosmos to be protected from the bad
entities.

The see-through entities symbolize the value placed on
truth. These entities can be seen straight through and thus
they cannot deceive. These see-through entities that fly
toward the dreamer are the rescuers or those that bring birth
or new life—for the dream is a birth fantasy that incorporates
the fetal bliss and ultimate protection of invisibility afforded

by the womb. The crystal tube in the shape and size of an index finger is the phallus that symbolically causes the impregnation. This brings the dreamer the beginning of a new life, as he becomes invisible.

Similarly, the see-through winged entities are a projection of the dreamer's transparency as he wishes to be entered—to be reborn within himself with light energy or cosmic seed entering his veins.

AN EXAMPLE OF PARALLEL DREAMING

The girlfriend of the above dreamer had a similar dream on the same night that he dreamt his dream of invisibility. The dreamers were apart during the dreaming, as the girlfriend was traveling. Therefore, the dreamers did not discuss their dreams until the following day. The girlfriend's dream is as follows:

> *I am on a plane. I am thinking that my friend is sick. The next thing I see is my friend in a hospital room. There are two doctors dressed in white by her side. They are putting liquid light through her wrist. They were worried that she may be depressed.*

Both dreams contain striking similarities: both dreamers are flying—one, on his own power, the other in a plane, the first dream has light beings administering some protective ingredient by touching the dreamer on his left wrist, while the other dream has doctors dressed in white performing a similar function: to enhance wellness they are putting liquid light through someone's wrist.

Interestingly, the dreamer of the first dream is visualized

as seeking protection from the evils of society. The dream depicts his need for connection to a nurturing force of goodness. The dreamer of the second dream may have sensed or been aware of her boyfriend's need for connection, flying parallel to his dream experience, as her sick friend may be none other than her boyfriend, whom the doctors are administering to—hooking him up to the liquid light of wellness, as he in his own dream simultaneously connects with a celestial umbilical cord.

The antecedent to the first dream may be the physical absence of the dreamer's girlfriend, as the dream reveals the dreamer's desire to be connected to an umbilical cord and thus a maternal or female element. What is important herein is the suggestion that the two dreamers were on the same unconscious wavelength. In other words, as the realm of unconsciousness is far greater than the realm of consciousness, there is shared unconsciousness in the dream world.

42

Cartoon Dreams

There is safety in dreaming of cartoons as the characters never die. Even after suffering unbelievable torments, the "toons" unflinchingly are ready for more of the same—fresh as new. The toons represent a celluloid hardiness, a plasticity, if you will, that allows them to bend and stretch and contort themselves into crazy shapes and sizes. They are fearless, as they believe in their own immortality. Dreams wherein cartoon characters play the major roles are hardly disguised because the visuals are disconnected from the emotional response. But one thing is clear, the very nature of animation is to bring life to a fearful or anxious idea that has not been given expression, a thought that has not been visually articulated. For animation imparts spirit and inspires actions; it takes a nondimensional thought and gives it the two-dimensional courage or resolution of a toon.

Dreaming of cartoon figures allows the dreamer to extend a fantasy all the way to death and back as the cartoon characters are omnipotent. This gives the dreamer the freedom to explore great kinetic energy without the emotional necessity these actions would cause. These moving illustrations of cartoon characters with their usually exaggerated physical features—such as the oversized heads that call attention to important facial expressions—are even more symbolic than the images of most dreams. A smile, a sneer, bulging eyes, or a grimace of grinding teeth quickly communicate or reveal the emotions of happiness, disgust, fear, or anger while oversized hands and feet stress the importance of the action. The following cartoon dream is a childhood dream that was dreamt by a former patient:

> *In this recurring dream I see an ostrich burying his head in the sand. I tell myself this is the ostrich from a cartoon that I watch all the time on television so definite am I that I had seen it. Yet when I awaken I am utterly frustrated that I can never identify the particular cartoon figure of my dream.*

The symbol of the ostrich burying his head in the sand cannot be more clear or revealing, as it signifies that there is something that the dreamer does not want to look at or remember. More specifically, the repellent sight is being hidden away under the sand along with the eyes of the ostrich, making vision or memory an impossibility. But there is no need to disguise this idea, as the cartoon ostrich is an animated omnipotent being that is far removed from the ego structure of the dreamer.

This is why the dreamer is able to casually state that she is definite that she had seen the action of this particular cartoon figure. Yet, the frustration of the dreamer (resulting from that which was seen and repressed) has been displaced away from the meaning of the dream to her annoyance over not being able to identify where she had seen this cartoon ostrich engage in a similar action. What is clear is that as a small child the dreamer had seen something that provided a negative stimulus. After several sessions the patient revealed that she had slept in the same room as her parents until the age of five, which means it was entirely possible that as an infant the dreamer, in the darkened room, may have witnessed her parents in the act of copulation.

43

Dreams of Dislocation
or Disorientation

Dreams of disorientation and dislocation are similar to the dream motif of losing things, however here what is lost or misplaced is the dreamer himself; somehow the internal compass of memory has led the dreamer astray on his well-traveled route. The dreamer may turn a familiar corner to find that his or her house is suddenly gone—replaced by the singular strangeness of a vacant lot! The dreamer, having inexplicably lost his or her bearings, experiences frightful anxiety and a profound sense of loss of control, a perceptive disequilibrium. Well-known material objects such as homes, cars, or edifices do not appear where they are supposed to be—in their proper locations—leaving the dreamer to stare blankly, in a state of confusion. Sometimes illogical transitions are made involving personages, such as a child who dreams in one instance of holding the hand of a parent only to look up and find that he or she is holding the hand of a stranger. The question remains—if these dreams strike terror in the hearts of all who dream them, why then are they dreamt? Let us examine the following dream of dislocation, which is somewhat less frightening than a dream of disorientation:

> *I walked into my apartment, a spacious well-lit room,*
> *and headed for my bedroom. I was shocked to see that*

*our car was in one corner of the room instead of my
bed. The car needed cleaning and to be looked over.
There were some rags lying around, and cleansers, as
though the car was ready to be cleaned.*

The well-lit apartment represents the fact that the dreamer
desires to delve into the darker areas of her unconscious. The
bedroom symbolizes the area of the heart, the emotions. The
car that is parked in one corner of the room where the bed
usually stands signifies that the dreamer has substituted her
bed for her car, or in other words, the bed is equated with her
car as that which is entered for purposes of relaxation and/or
excitation. But whereas the car takes the dreamer away from
the home and represents freedom, the bed keeps the dreamer
at home, or bedridden. To be bedridden is feared, as it represents inactivity and sleep (or death), which is why the object
of fear is removed from its usual habitat and replaced with
the object of desire that represents movement, energy, and
speed, the sought after attributes—the revved-up motors of
vitality. Therefore the car must be preserved, its motor kept
running (like the beating of a heart). Thus, by substituting the
car for the bed, the dreamer thwarts off the fear of death by
incorporating into her psyche the drive to live.

Disorienting dreams momentarily upset the emotional stability or equilibrium of the dreamer. For the most part these
dreams express self-doubt, the fear that one will make the
wrong judgment or will not be able to get to where one is
going, or finalize what one wants to achieve. These dreams
represent the unconscious frustration of dreamers who feel
thwarted in their attempts to progress—in their attempts to
find what they are looking for. The dreamer may believe him
or herself to be blocked or at an impasse in life. The validity

of perception is criticized. The following dream is typically disorienting:

> *It is early morning. I am walking to school concerned about arriving late as I am afraid I will miss a test. I walk down the usual three blocks and start the incline. I walk up this long block to the end of the street from where my High School usually comes into view. But to my horror, the school is gone. I look all around but cannot find my school. I ask someone on the street but they do not seem to know where the school is. I look at the street sign and it is correct so I have not made an error. I start to panic and then I awake.*

The horror of this dream comes from the realization that one cannot depend on anything, even oneself—for one's own dependability comes under attack. The dreamer begins to chastise herself for being late which in turn discredits her sense of responsibility. Knowledge is called into question, as no one knows where the school is. A stranger is called upon to validate the dreamer's perception, to take blame away from the dreamer. The street sign is found to be correct as a means of assuring the dreamer that she is not inept, that she has not made a mistake. The problem of remembering or the lack thereof is deftly externalized onto situational or environmental factors so as to preserve the dreamer's sense of self-worth. The dreamer panics for more reasons than that she will miss her test—she panics because she is aware of impermanence and loss. The dream is a wake-up call not to take anything for granted, as it pragmatically reveals the transience of life—what is here today may be gone tomorrow.

44

Synecdoche Dreams

Synecdoche dreams are dreams that utilize a part of something for a whole, where the part symbolically designates the whole: such as the use of the term ''hired hands'' for ''men'' or as in the phrase ''a face that launched a thousand ships.'' Among inanimate objects the word ''table'' is used in the phrase ''she set a nice table'' to represent the meaning of the whole dinner. Using a part for a whole focuses attention on a detail, thereby stressing the importance of that particular feature, for example: the substitution of ''vicious tongues'' for ''detractors'' emphasizes oral treachery. The synecdoche often personifies objects by making an abstraction concrete. The synecdoche is used in dreams as a means of ideational condensation. The following dream was dreamt by a former patient:

> *I was near the ocean, walking alone on the shore. No one else was around. I was feeling cold. The wind was blowing. I put on the weather beaten brown leather jacket I was carrying with me. I put my arms into the sleeves and zipped it up. I felt warmer.*

The dream contains all the visuals of loneliness and isolation. The external weather being cold is a reflection of the dreamer's inner sense of emotional chill. (It must be noted that the brown leather jacket in the dream is one that actually belongs to the dreamer's husband who, in the last year of their marriage, had become extremely distant and aloof.) By substituting the jacket for the husband the dreamer is able to symbolically put the husband's arms (in the guise of the jacket) around her in a protective embrace. The only way the dreamer can derive some feeling of emotional warmth is by wearing the husband's jacket, where the jacket is a synecdoche for the unavailable and distant husband. By carrying the jacket the dreamer feels in some way connected to the husband. By wearing the jacket the dreamer bonds with her husband in a wished-for unity.

45

Movie Dreams

A movie dream is viewed as an aesthetic whole with a beginning and an end. The dream is perceived as though the dreamer were a viewer watching his or her own performance. In other words, this is a dream of *perceptual participation* wherein we feel our own presence. There is constant movement and *the movement is always perceived as real*. And there is highly elaborated action of which the dreamer is the focal point. Often the scenes have an ordered sequence of events as in a real movie wherein the dreamer sits back and says "let's see what happens." Most important, these dreams are not about an isolated incident but rather about a broad conception of the way things are. They give a vivid impression of reality and are thematic in form. The following dream of **Luciano Pavarotti** (see problem-solving dreams) is repeated herein, as it contains a movie motif:

> *I was at the movies watching Orson Welles playing Othello. I was in the audience when suddenly I took Orson Welles' place. I was watching myself playing the role of Orson Welles, a hero of mine, thinking this is very presumptuous of me because Orson Welles is such a great actor.*

Although Pavarotti first perceives himself as part of the audience and thus, *detached,* he makes the transition from the movie seat of the objective viewer to the screen image of the subjective performer by *actively participating* in the movie. By taking Orson's place on the screen he is literally *watching himself watching himself* to feel his own presence and learn from this self-referential experience.

In the following dream **June LeBell,** on-air personality on WQXR FM Radio, *is* the movie herself (which could be entitled, *The CD From Hell),* viewed by an audience of forty-four men:

> *Forty-three Japanese men had come to view all the technology at WQXR. Herb Squire, the CEO, was taking them on a tour. In the next scene, I am trying to get a new CD player to work, but in order to get anything to play I need to enter an algebraic formula and equation. My announcer's script stated the music and times but when I announced "this was Beethoven" it was Shubert, and when I announced that the piece was fifteen minutes it was thirty minutes long. Nothing was working correctly, and the timing was wrong. I had the voice of the chief announcer Duncan Pirnie on tape (who was supposed to recap) but I couldn't get his voice to play, and I couldn't imitate him. My boss and the forty-three Japanese men were outside watching me from behind the glass wall; the Japanese giggled behind their hands. I pressed a button on the left side of the control room and the machine on the right side began to play. Nothing worked. Everything went wrong.*

Once again this is a performance-anxiety, cinematic dream that involves watching and being watched. The dreamer, aware of being watched by her boss—the critical introspective superego—is also given external negative feedback by the forty-three Japanese men giggling behind the glass. The control room not working signifies that the dreamer feels a loss of control. The phrase "behind the glass" signifies that the dreamer is getting a behind-the-scenes look at herself: the self-referential element, perhaps the role of a "techie," is one the dreamer cannot imitate.

PART III

Actualized
Dreams

Unlike a dream that occurs in our unconscious minds during periods of deep sleep, an actualized dream occurs during consciousness, with our eyes wide open. It is defined as *an extreme act,* a deliberate *behavioral* acting out of a fantasy during consciousness, wherein the unconscious aim is to fulfill an instinctual desire or wish. An actualized dream can be visualized as an escaped id that has just locked the door on the superego (our conscience) in an attempt to permit an unconscionable behavioral act to occur, an act that would surely be sublimated or suppressed (forbidden) in the world of consciousness. It is theorized that such a behavioral act, which I have termed an *actualized dream,* may be given psychoanalytic interpretation much in the same manner as dream analysis. (See actualized dream interpretations of John F. Kennedy Jr.; Diana, Princess of Wales; President Bill Clinton; Michael Jackson; King Edward VIII, etc.).

As "sleep" dreams have a moral purpose such as consolation, repudiation, rebuke, or self-affirmation, so must the "wakeful," actualized dream. But whereas a dream is a passive internal expression of unconscious fulfillments—making known what has been repressed in the unconscious—the actualized dream is active, unrepressed, externally expressed, *and it takes place during consciousness.* The action has motive and is a meaningful representation of failed repression. What is behind the wakeful action, the behavior, the image ought in theory to be analyzed in the same manner as a dream, as the ''actualized dreamer'' is the dream itself and thus the symbolic content. The narrative has been discarded for the purely visual.

The cause of the extreme action may be found in the psycho-emotional disposition of ''the actualizer'' (herein John F. Kennedy Jr.; Diana, Princess of Wales, etc.). This disposition is a result of the individual's psychic past. Events, such as the assassination of President Kennedy, or the philandering of Prince Charles, that trigger strong emotional responses leave heavy-handed imprints on thoughts and actions.

The actualized dream is the opposite of a sleep dream that realizes or fulfills a wish in the unconscious world of fantasy. *This is a fantasy realized or fulfilled in conscious reality.* And unlike a dream, the actualized dream can be reproduced and remembered with accuracy. The reason behind the act may or may not be understood by the actualizer, in that an action supersedes the thought behind it. Every action is motivated from the wish that something should or should not happen—as the action is the struggle for the realization of a wish. But one must first examine the purpose of an action and what effect it is supposed to have. As the action is the aftereffect of the cause—the shock waves after an earthquake—the action should reveal the seismic shift beneath the fault line, the malaise beneath the symptom.

Like a sleep dream, the actualized dream rectifies a situation, but it does so not only by symbolic expression but by physical manifestation in the realm of visual consciousness. Therefore, nothing is expressed in disguised form, nothing is hidden—*what you see is what you get.* The following are examples of actualized dreams.

46

John F. Kennedy Jr.

John F. Kennedy Jr. poses naked for photographers in sexually explicit positions and has photos printed in the January 1998 Esquire *magazine. One such photo displays Kennedy bending from the rear; another photo has the buff Kennedy spread-eagled on the floor sporting a sleeveless T-shirt cropped above the navel—the T-shirt is labeled Cuban Missile Crisis with a black arrow pointing downward toward the phallus.*

THE SIGNIFICANCE OF PHYSICAL SYMBOLIC PRESENTATION

John Kennedy's behavioral act—appearing naked in *Esquire*—is his actualized dream. His nakedness is the dream symbol. The interpretation is as follows: The wish to reveal or expose oneself translates into the ardent desire to show the body alive and vital, and is viewed as a symbol of individuation, wherein one needs to feel individuated. The nakedness reveals the totality of the psyche or being, the identity, the wholeness of self, and may be considered a revelation—for what is wholly personal becomes openly public. A peek through a keyhole is telescopically expanded to encompass the heavens. But the need for individuation is more than just the wish for self-disclosure. The wish for exposure is based on a fear of castration so immense that the body itself has become the phallus. In other words, *the castration fear has metastasized into the fear of annihilation:* the fear of castration demands that the genitalia be exposed to unsuspecting passersby to prove to the world that castration has *not* taken place; the fear of annihilation necessitates that the exhibitionist reveal his whole self (viewed as a phallus) to prove that he is alive, and not dead. (This would suggest that JFK Jr. has internalized his dead father.)

The wish to expose oneself is also viewed as a symbol of regression (the desire to return to an earlier form of functioning and existence where feelings of omnipotence and grandiosity are revived)—the exhibitionist is as naked as the day he was born. (The assassination trauma is replaced with the bringing forth of a new life, as nakedness is often a symbol of rebirth.) The photo of Kennedy bending from the rear reveals an adolescent naughtiness—it manifests a childish need to assume a "kiss my ass" defiant stance, and is deemed regressive.

Although his guard is seemingly down, Kennedy's exposure/actualized dream may be seen as a defensive act that is protective in nature; John is guarding his existence from the threat of annihilation by assassination. Indeed, his is a frontal assault. It is assumed that the incendiary photos will prevent him from running for the office of the presidency, and from suffering the same fate as his father. The photos clearly symbolize Kennedy *running from office.* Thus, John's actualized dream does more than just bare his soul; the actualized dream rips up the presidential ticket and eliminates the repetition trauma of the assassination.

John's actualized dream may also be viewed as a symbol of hostility toward his father. As children typically have the notion of being betrayed by the parent who dies, they often seek to betray the betrayer in return. John's in-your-face photographs are a reparation of sorts, particularly the photo where he wears nothing but a Cuban missile crisis T-shirt with an arrow pointing downward toward his phallus. The downward arrow symbolically cries, ''I'm explosive . . . I'm the missile that is about to go off.'' Pouf! In the snap of a photograph, nothing more is left to the imagination, where what is imagined is more threatening than what is known and perceived.

Lastly, the actualized dream symbolizes Kennedy's wish to get to the bottom of what actually happened on that fateful day in November, for he does not know the truth; he only knows the maddening cover-up. As truth is associated with becoming naked, he uncovers himself in the wish that his nakedness will bring forth a similar clarification. The deadly attack, hypothesized as coming from behind the grassy knoll, was never in view; what happened was never fully perceived. Thus, the actualized dream hides nothing, as everything is left bare. This is the trade-off wish for demystification.

47

Diana,
Princess of Wales

Shortly after Christmas, January 1982, the three-months-pregnant Diana, Princess of Wales, throws herself down a wooden flight of stairs in front of her retreating husband, Prince Charles. (Diana, Her True Story by Andrew Morton, New York: Simon & Schuster, 1992)

THE SIGNIFICANCE OF PHYSICAL PRESENTATION

Here, the actualized dream of Princess Diana permits an unconscionable act—Princess Diana throws herself down the stairs in a symbolic attempt to descend the throne of England. The act is the opposite of ascending the throne or of royal ascension in general. The loss of footing symbolizes that Diana has lost her emotional foothold in marriage. The actualized dream occurs on a flight of stairs, which reveals the wish for flight, to flee from her distressful situation. The stairs symbolize the wish for all to see, as ''stairs'' is a phonetic rendering of *stares*.

The actualized dream occurs during pregnancy because the pregnancy has become a physical symbol of a psychological state of anxiety—the Princess has been emotionally violated, tampered with. The pregnancy also symbolizes a pregnant pause, an uncomfortable silence, a hiatus in her love relationship. The wish of the actualized dream is to sever ties, to detach the placenta from the umbilical cord, to eliminate any royal connection. Diana, symbolically tied to the baby within, identifies herself with an innocence that Charles has already done away with. By deliberately throwing herself down the stairs and thereby risking miscarriage, Diana's actualized dream symbolizes the following message—"there is no room for the both of us, one must be killed off"—a reference to Camilla, mistress of the philandering Charles. Similarly, the miscarriage—viewed as the underlying wish of the actualized dream action—symbolizes a miscarriage of justice. The miscarriage, in turn, would rob Prince Charles of his heir, which has the phonetic rendering of air, meaning his breath. Finally, Diana would take his breath away!

Throwing herself down the stairs symbolizes Diana in the throws of emotional difficulty. Thrown off track, she is lacking in judgment. Throwing herself in the direction of the retreating Charles is the actualized dream's attempt at displacement, as Diana would like to displace her misery onto her husband. By replacing the word "throwing" with "hurling," we are reminded of Diana's bulimia, her numerous throw-ups symbolizing the wish to rid herself of something distasteful, something that cannot be tolerated, of her wish to get something out of her system.

48

President Bill Clinton

President Bill Clinton is given oral sex by an aid, Monica Lewinsky, in the Oval Office of the White House, the threat of being caught ever present.

THE SIGNIFICANCE OF PHYSICAL SYMBOLIC PRESENTATION

President Clinton's extreme behavioral act—having oral sex in the Oval Office of the White House—is his actualized dream. The Oval Office is the dream symbol. A house that encloses the individual usually symbolizes the self or the personality. The grander the house, the more powerful the sense of self. Thus, living in the White House has made Clinton feel invincible.

In that a room often symbolizes the womb, the Oval office, by virtue of its shape, is a definite womb substitute. Therefore, any sucking activity that occurs in this room can be interpreted as a regressive act (returning to an earlier phase of development where emphasis is on bodily satisfaction particularly of oral nature). This is the wish to return to the womb where the fetus sucks or feeds off the maternal umbilicus (the umbilical cord). But, by reversal, Bill substitutes the sucking need with the need to be sucked. As regression also vivifies narcissistic feelings of omnipotence and grandiosity, caution is thrown to the wind. Clinton's needs are gratified without any thought of the ramifications, in that engaging in oral sex disguises his real desire. *Entering the Oval Room to have sex symbolically means entering the mother.*

The White House in all its grandeur symbolizes ultimate supremacy, the power of the maternal figure over the dependent nursing child, for the White House signifies the house of milk, the house that represents the act of being nurtured and given sustenance, the house that signifies the substance of life.

The threat of getting caught is overriden by the wish to stay attached to the mother, for the fetus is literally caught up inside the mother. The excitement and danger involved in maneuvering this actualized dream to occur (the blow job in the Oval Office) is also tied to a fear of castration by the father, (or, in this case, the one that wears the pants in the family). Thus, by having sex in the Oval Room—the womb substitute—Bill fulfills the oedipal fantasy, for this is the room where the fathering is done. *And he proves that he has not been castrated by Hillary.*

49

Michael Jackson

Michael Jackson becomes white and undergoes extensive facial reconstruction through plastic surgery.

THE SIGNIFICANCE OF PHYSICAL SYMBOLIC PRESENTATION

Michael Jackson's actualized dream is the action of turning from black to white. The dream symbol is one of transformation wherein Michael undergoes a physical change and thus presents himself in a new manner, a new metamorphosis—like a snake sloughs its old covering, he emerges *in new skin.*

The radical change in appearance may be symbolized as changing colors or changing sides. In other words, Michael is escaping his past, he has found a way out of his skin.

The extensive facial surgery is another symbol of becoming someone different, for taking on a new persona denies and nullifies the old Michael. This is a way of disowning the past. As radical changes in physical appearance usually occur in sexually abused children or children who are traumatically overstimulated—in children who have had their sense of identity interfered with—Michael's actualized dream is indeed viewed as a defense against recognition, both physical and mental.

50

King Edward VIII
(Duke of Windsor)

King Edward VIII abdicates the throne of England on December 11, 1936, to marry the divorcée Wallis Simpson.

THE SIGNIFICANCE OF PHYSICAL SYMBOLIC PRESENTATION

King Edward VIII's extreme act, of abdicating the throne of England, is his actualized dream. The throne and England are the dream symbols. With England symbolizing the motherland, or mother country, Edward's abdication is an act against his mother, Queen Mary. The throne, as the seat of power, symbolizes the toilet. Leaving the toilet represents an unwilling child—an anal retentive (obstinate and defiant) personality. The abdication is the sublimation of Edward's anal character and reflects an obstinancy in Edward's nature—a willful reaction against the demands made by other people.

Taking into account that during the anal stage (early stage) of development, children tend to view their bowel movements or feces as a gift to their mothers, it is believed that the feces is seen as a part of themselves and viewed as a personal sacrifice. It is interesting, therefore, that Edward

holds back, as he does not make the sacrifice, does not relin-
quish his love, Wallis Simpson, the divorcée. (Wallis signifies what has been divorced—as the feces from the body—
thus, Edward does not give her up.)

The abdication means that Edward does not intend to give
a part of himself to England, the mother substitute, and it
represents the ultimate expression of a defiance typical in
anal retentives. Symbolically, the actualized dream suggests
that King Edward will not do his duties!

Yet, Edward's actualized dream may also symbolize an
anal-erotic character trait where pleasure is attached to the
function of evacuation. Here, the evacuation is fulfilled when
Edward leaves England in self-imposed exile.

51

Jocelyne Wildenstein

Jocelyne Wildenstein has extensive facial surgery to make herself look like a lion. (George Holz photo appeared in the December 15, 1997, issue of New York *magazine.)*

THE SIGNIFICANCE OF PHYSICAL SYMBOLIC PRESENTATION

Jocelyne's behavioral act—altering her facial features to achieve the inhuman image of a cat—is her actualized dream. Choosing to look like an endangered species, specifically the lion, is the dream symbol. The interpretation is as follows: The wish to alter one's appearance to the point of loss of recognition symbolizes the need for transformation and can be seen as an attempt to nullify a present situation or state of being. Giving oneself the features of a wild beast is a desperate attempt to gain power. It must be noted that Jocelyne is the estranged wife of Alec Wildenstein, one of the world's richest art collectors and owner of Wildenstein Gallery in New York City. (Alec has left her for another woman.) It also must be noted that Jocelyne had first met her husband, formerly an avid hunter, during a lion hunt at Ol Jogi, his family ranch in Kenya. It also bears mentioning that

Alec is now a wild game conservationist. Keeping these facts in mind will allow us to interpret Jocelyne's actualized dream as the wish for the preservation or conservation of her marriage, as she is now the very beast her husband is seeking to protect.

The transition from hunter to conservationist marks a symbolic change in her husband's attitude: ownership is no longer important, the chase has lost its seductive value. Similarly, what was once sought after (as Jocelyne formerly was) and trapped is no longer violated, but given its freedom. Therefore, Jocelyne's actualized dream seeks to stimulate once again Alec's waning passion to collect the wild, the rare, and the unobtainable—the exotic species that she had become. After all, she has violated herself through surgery and therefore opts for captivity.

In other words, the one thing the Wildensteins still have in common is their love of Africa and things wild—thus, Jocelyne becomes a wild thing. Her disfiguring surgery is viewed as a manifestation of her wild and impassioned nature in the hopes that once exposed, this nature will inevitably prove attractive to Mr. Wildenstein.

Similarly, becoming a lion has the unmistakable value of giving Jocelyne the upper hand, as it imbues her with a powerful presence whose essence is not fully understood. Because Jocelyne has physically transcended the human realm and has entered the realm of the beast, she is no longer a fathomable entity and may thus be able to fascinate, to awe her bored husband. Her facial transfiguration reveals the extent of her alienation from humanity. The idea of divorce may have shattered Jocelyne's ego to the point where she may no longer be able to compete on a human level.

Yet, Jocelyne's extreme act may be considered one of

self-preservation, for it is the lioness that does the killing, the lioness that has been termed a noble beast. She has after all lionized herself in her own eyes.

Lastly, the name Wildenstein has symbolic significance in that the word "wild" is encased within it. The word "stein" means mug in German, and "face" in British slang. By being a "wild face" Mrs. Wildenstein retains her married name by physically embodying and personifying it, which is her hidden desire. This symbolically suggests that Jocelyne will always be a Wildenstein, even more so than Mr. Wildenstein.

52

The Hitlerian
Goose Step

The goose-stepping motion is used by the Nazi foot soldiers.

THE SIGNIFICANCE OF PHYSICAL SYMBOLIC PRESENTATION

The actualized dream is the wish that a country will be able to kick everything out of the way—to kick over the future with its raised demoralizing boot. The symbol is the sadistic element present in the kicking action of the foot meant to dehumanize the recipient.

In the goose step there is no raising of the knee as in a normal walk; the normal walk has a backward movement inherent in the motion. The forward thrust of the legs (in the goose step) symbolizes a mind firmly fixed on future domination, a mind that does not look back at the past, a conquering mind that focuses on encroaching outward—where retreat is not a possibility.

There is no bending or flexibility at the knee and this represents an uncompromising philosophy: there is no plasticity to the model, no acquiescence. The knee is locked into its own stiffness and symbolizes an autocratic nature and the rigidity of the Nazi mentality. All at once the whole foot comes down flat on the ground, as opposed to the normal descent of heel followed by toe, so there is no escape of whatever is underfoot; whatever is not kicked is crushed.

Because of the motion of the goose step, an emphasis is placed on the lower portion of the body—as in the animal species—which suggests that the brain is less important. The feet are the dominant motif.

The upward and forward thrust of the stiffened leg becomes a phallic symbol—a penile erection in need of penetration: the annexing of Austria, the transgression into France, etc. are representations of male domination.

53

Howard Hughes

Howard Hughes becomes reclusive and walks around with tissue boxes on his feet as slippers, and carries wads of tissues in his hand so he never has to touch anything directly.

THE SIGNIFICANCE OF PHYSICAL SYMBOLIC PRESENTATION

In that the billionaire recluse Howard Hughes walked around in pajamas, wore tissue boxes on his feet, held wads of tissues in his hands so he would not touch anything directly because he was afraid of germs, his actualized dream symbolized an excessive need to stay clean. The tissue is the symbol. But in that the tissues would pick up germs on whatever he touched, it seemed his wish was to acquire, collect, and hold onto his germs, where money may have been symbolically equated with germs, as in dirty money. Similarly, as money passes through many hands, Mr. Hughes refused to let himself be touched by any human hand. Indeed, Mr. Hughes may have seen himself as money, as the physical embodiment of money.

Furthermore, as the tissue is a symbol of where one blows one's nose—a place where germs are disposed of—the issue behind the tissue is that Hughes thought of himself as a germ. For after all, he was cutting himself and everyone else off from himself (most likely out of guilt). His reclusive act, therefore, seems to suggest that he believed that he would infect others, as his act was deliberately masochistic and self-punishing, an act that resulted in his death from liver failure, the organ that rids the body of impurities!

These are but a few examples of what I have termed actualized dreams. There are many more. In conclusion, the main advantage of interpreting a physical action is that it allows individuals to understand their behavior more fully, to learn how their behavior is a reflection of thoughts that may be unconscious. The act of analyzing an action allows the actualizer to distance him or herself from the act. This distance is needed for objectivity—*which is why one must leave the self in order to learn the self.*

Another actualized dream that bears brief mentioning is the transatlantic flight of **Charles Lindbergh.** The action of the non–stop flight symbolically suggests that Lindbergh wanted to prove that he could go the distance. We can all go the distance if we start being clever with ourselves.

PART IV

Demystification

54

Decoding Your Dream

BASIC STEPS

1. Always write down what you were doing the day before the dream (the day residue or antecedent).

2. Always establish the locale of the dream and the time frame.

3. Establish character delineation (who plays whom); remember that you may be more than one character in your dream regardless of gender or species.

4. Categorize your dream into one of the nine types.

5. Look for your dream motif.

6. Establish your emotional state (glad, sad, guilty, frightened, jealous, angry, frustrated).

7. Circle all symbols in pen (boat, sun, table, tree, etc.), and on a separate paper, copy down the symbols and place equal signs next to them. Then define what they mean to you—*think associations.*

8. Examine the wording and underline any cliché.

9. Look for any phonetic associations (blue/blew; chased/chaste).

10. Look at names of individuals who may represent others with the same name; notice initials as well, including the initials of objects, particularly if the object, image, or symbol does not mean anything to you. For example, that big box in your dream may only be there to represent the initials B. B., which might be the initials of your ex-boyfriend or girlfriend.

11. Watch for distortions (wherein something is given major importance instead of minimalized), projections (wherein the subject of a proposition becomes transposed with the object—in other words, wherein we make someone else feel about us what we feel about them, e.g., *"I love you"* becomes *"you love me"),* reaction formations (wherein the predicate of the proposition is transposed into its opposite, e.g., *"I love you"* becomes *"I hate you"),* displacements (wherein something becomes something else), reversals (wherein order or logic is reversed), or word play (wherein names have hidden meanings).

55

Dream
Analyses

M any times the interpretation or demystification of a dream is as simple as finding the dream cliché, as the cliché often reveals the theme of the dream. The theme of the dream is useful at first, as it starts the interpretation walking in the right direction. However, the final destination may be one that was not at first imaginable. The following is an example of a dream that makes wonderful use of cliché. But as we shall see, what starts out as an anxiety dream turns into a dream of self-affirmation. I interpreted the dream live over the air on *The Joey Reynolds Show* while I was Joey's "dream" guest, analyzing the dreams of call-ins. The woman dreamer validated my interpretation. Here is the dream in its entirety:

DREAM 1 (with cliché)

I was upstairs in the hallway of the building that I work in, after hours. There was this glass partition in front of me. On the other side a lion was slowly pacing from one side of the floor to the other. I was frightened. Suddenly the glass doors open and the lion starts moving towards me. It gets closer and closer. <u>I'm up against the wall.</u> But when the lion reaches me it gently licks my nose.

Dream Analysis 1

I have deliberately underlined the cliché "I'm up against the wall," because it establishes the theme of the dream as one of helplessness wherein the dreamer feels that she has reached an impasse. This categorizes the dream as being one of classic anxiety and suggests that in *actuality* our dreamer may also be feeling *up against a wall*—as though she has reached some stalemate where she cannot progress further. As this was determined to be the case, it is significant for us to make note of how this frustrating feeling has manifested itself in terms of cliché, and how the dream has employed symbolism as its translator of emotions. But as we shall see, the intention of the dream is to convince the dreamer that her situation is far from helpless . . . as there are options that she has left unexplored.

We must focus on the locale of the dream. It is helpful to know that the woman is at her place of "work," and that she is there "after hours" as this metaphorically alludes to the fact that the woman takes her work home with her at night. Thus, it is not inappropriate to assume that the anxiety presented within the dream may be work-related.

The "lion" that majestically strides along the hallway seems to *own the hallway,* and therefore represents a figure of authority such as a boss or an employer. The lion may also be a symbolic representation of the lion icon of the Dreyfus fund, which is associated with "financial security," a work-related theme.

Yet, the lion does no harm. Perhaps its growl is

worse than its bite. For, in what can be deemed a significant gesture, the lion affectionately licks the
dreamer's nose as though the lion were a pet dog.
(Here we should note that the lion has been defused. It
may as well have been symbolically reduced to the size
of a dog in that it acts like a dog.) This means that the
dream holds a special wish—to calm or tame the savage beast that oppresses our dreamer. Because the
dream contains the wish to turn the oppressor into the
oppressed, and because the woman successfully holds
her ground by giving herself the presence of mind or
seductive ability necessary to be able to succeed at
such an awesome task, we now realize that this is no
ordinary anxiety dream but rather a dream of wish fulfillment and self-affirmation in which the woman
dreamer will awaken from the dream experience feeling relieved and with renewed spirit.

The glass partition symbolizes a delineation of
space and the sense of opposition or separation, and
suggests the two-sided nature of the situation or relationship. The glass symbolizes the dreamer's attempt
to see what is really happening—perhaps the wish to
see behind closed doors, or to gain access to information one is not privy to. But the glass partition views
both ways and so may symbolize the dreamer's wish to
be seen (working overtime) and certainly to be noticed
and even rewarded for her effort (which comes in the
form of the lion's affectionate lick). Most important,
the glass partition has allowed the dreamer to view her
options in a more positive manner. As all the dream
symbols are related to a work situation we may say that
the analysis is a good narrational fit.

The dreamer concurred with the interpretation, as she was now able to understand the dream's message and thus its aim. The following two dreams of friends illustrate the creative nature of the dream world and highlight the devious conduct of the unconscious mind—its use of disguises and subterfuge, such as displacement, reversal, and distortion:

DREAM 2 (where reversal takes place)

I am in my living room. To the left, seated on the sofa, is Jacqueline Onassis (in actuality, she is already deceased). I greet her and extend my sympathy in regards to her loss of her loved one, Maurice Tempelsman. I tell her "I am so sorry." She is looking at an empty chair across from where she is seated. I try to console her with the words, "I'm sure he is with you right now, in fact, I'm sure he is seated in this empty chair." She smiles sweetly and agrees, saying, "Yes, I know that."

Dream Analysis 2

Of primary importance to the interpretation of this dream is the realization that a profound *reversal* of situation has occurred—the deceased Jacqueline is now the bereaved companion; the grieving companion, Maurice, is now the deceased. The reversal establishes the wish of the dream: that things be different from how they are in actuality, but also allows the process of displacement to distort reality in a way that is favorable to the emotions of our dreamer, for with Jacqueline alive the dreamer may share Jacqueline's feelings of loss, her suffering and sense of loneliness. This translates to: I feel for *her,* not *him* . . . because *he* left her. This emphatic spirit becomes more relevant when we take into consideration our dreamer's former identification with Jacqueline Onassis, which suggests that Jacqueline is a representation of the dreamer. Now that the dreamer has become distanced enough from herself to assume the persona of someone else she is better equipped to recognize her sorrow and the emptiness of her emotional life.

Because our dreamer states that she is in her living room, death has undergone a transformation and become a live and present entity. Life, however, has been symbolically represented through its opposite—an empty chair, upon which the emptiness of the dreamer's life metaphorically rests.

The symbol of the empty chair has great significance, as it often represents a loved one who is no longer reachable. How fitting, then, that the initials of Maurice Tempelsman are *M. T.*, which, when vocalized, have the phonetic meaning of *empty.*

In that the dream is formulated on an *initial reversal* of reality, it may contain yet another reversal of just that—an *initial* reversal. For by reversing Mr. Tempelsman's initials we are confronted with the letters *T* and *M,* which signify the initials of the long lost friend that the dreamer had been longing to see. Therefore, the dream wish may be viewed as one of self-consolation, wherein the dreamer has comforted herself with the idea that she is not alone, that her friend is with her in his thoughts and in his heart.

DREAM 3 (with displacement, distortion and word play)

I am riding in a horse-drawn carriage to an old stone house that belongs to my father. I am supposed to be meeting him there, but the house is empty. I walk through the house and it begins to start crumbling. Suddenly I get stuck in a stone wall, as if I melt into the wall. I am inside the wall and I cannot get out.

Dream Analysis 3

As houses represent the being and the personality, an old stone house reflects an older person who is perceived as being emotionally cold, hard, and immovable. (One cannot get blood from a stone.) In that the house belongs to our dreamer's father, the house *is* the father that the dreamer would like to walk through and explore. Similarly, the meeting symbolizes the dreamer's desire to connect with or reach his father. But the father's absence from the home represents the dreamer's difficulty in defining his father even on a conceptual level.

There is also the fear that the sad recognition of the father's inaccessibility will bring punishment upon our dreamer, which is why the house begins crumbling. Yet the wish of our dreamer to identify or forge a relationship with his father is so intense that he becomes a part of the wall in the house, a part of his father. His getting stuck in a wall literally forces a consolidation between dreamer and father. The great focus on the wall is an attempt at distortion, because the wall is a symbolic representation of his father—as the father has been displaced onto the wall. But as we shall see, our dreamer's creative use of word play makes possible our dreamer's goal of becoming a part of his father. (It is necessary to know that in Greek the name of the dreamer's father is Panos, which has the English translation of "all." Interestingly, the word "all" is contained within the word wall which means that the dreamer is *within* his father to the extent that in his dream he is the wall.)

PART V

Dream
Symbols

56

How to Interpret Dream Symbols

The following list of dream symbols may be used as a guide to help you interpret your own dream symbols. This list can make no claim, however, to an exclusivity of meaning. This is because dream symbols are complex entities that are literally more than meets the eye, and thus open to subjective interpretation. Each symbol, therefore, must be analyzed as it applies to each specific dream, where the very meaning of a symbol may change or become modified by its relationship to the dream narrative as a whole, to the dream motif, and by how it corresponds with the other symbols within the dream text.

Clearly, in regard to inanimate objects like mirrors that reflect or windows that open, or environmental features such as oceans and trees, there is a certain degree of universal meaning. However, even here we are faced with the possibility that many well-known objects are emotionally loaded symbols for specific individuals.

A passage in Jung's *Dreams* reminds us about the dreamer who dreamt of a table. Jung informs us that this seemingly unambiguous table was one that had particular significance for the dreamer as this was *the* table at which the dreamer's father sat when he chastised his son for being a wastrel and cut him off financially, which had the effect of forever making the table an unpleasant symbol of the son's worthlessness. This passage also reveals how life situations are remembered and recorded by the brain as if they are audiovisual scenes that were shot for a movie—scenes that incorporate the whole picture, the environment, the images, the moving figures, and the dialogue that determine the mood of the situation.

This is why when we reflect on our dreams we must remember that our dreams have been recalled from our past, a past laden with symbols that are temporarily meaningful. We must define our dream symbols and make appropriate associations and be satisfied with the fact that there can be no wrong dream interpretations, for each interpretation represents a certain level of personal understanding, and thus a hidden part of our self that is now revealed.

DREAM SYMBOLS

Above: consciousness

Aisle: pathway, walking down the aisle, spiritual bonding, vows, commitment, dedication or purpose; (phonetic—I'll: assertion)

Alien: a deceased being, one who feels alienated

Animal: religious or spiritual being, instinctual nature

Arch, Archway: rite of passage

Architectural structures: body parts

Arms: protection, embracing love, (phonetic—alms: gifts given in charitable spirit)

At sea: not on solid ground, without understanding

Awakening: recognition, illumination

Baby: achievement, body of work, creation, creative process

Background: past life

Back seat: being driven, not in control

Backstage: the unconscious

Backyard: your own turf

Ball: sphere, world, self-concept, as point around which everything revolves

Barefoot: baring one's soul, getting in touch with the earth, instinctual nature

Basement: the unconscious

Bathroom: relief, cleansing, bathroom stall, begging for time

Beach: encampment, solitude, peace

Beasts: individuation, breaking away from norms, animal instincts

Behind: past

Below: the unconscious

Bench: permanence, inactivity, to keep from moving

Bikini-clad woman: the anima (female element in male unconscious, goddess as guide)

Black dog: instinctual desires, symbol of foreboding death (emotional or physical)

Blanket: security, comfort, protection

Blind: lack of vision, foresight, faith

Blue: the unknown (into the blue), truth, spirituality, sadness; (phonetic—blew: gone)

Boat: foundation of life, conveyance, boat arrival, rite of passage

Book: of life, self-discovery, pages unread within the dreamer, gospel

Bridges: connections to another world, level of understanding

Briefcase: a philosophy of ideas

Bright lights: fame, blindness, exposure

Broken window: self destruction, emotional upheaval, inner turmoil

Bugs: babies

Building: the self, creative impulses, constructive outlook

Bunk: unification, steadfastness

Bushes: subterfuge, concealment, submerged sexual urges, genitalia

Calling card: sense of identity

Camel: beast of burden, responsibility

Camp: staying entrenched in youthful exuberance and spirit

Candles: optimism, illumination

Car: drive; inside a specific world

Cartoon: omnipotence

Cashier, Check-out people: being checked out, taken stock of; adding things up

Castle: the body; loftier, mature sense of self

Caverns: female genitalia

Ceiling: limiting factor

Chair: permanence, solidity

Chalk lines: death, looking for answers

Chased: sense of being pursued; (phonetic—chaste: morally and ethically pure, modest)

Circle: concept of self, totality, wholeness, timelessness, continuance, mandala

Cities: symbolic of dreamer

Climbing (or climbing stairs): sexual activity

Collapsing: sexual culmination

College course: the course of life, learning, introspection

Columns: body, or body parts, phallic symbol, standing tall, supportive, upholding ideals, order

Conductor: energizer, conduit, one who runs things

Corners: the four points of reference in the world, totality, wholeness

Costume: disguise, deception, roles we assume

Coverings: layers of memory

Crib: safety zone, protection

Crumpling: sexual culmination

Dancing: sexual activity

Darkness: ambivalence

Datebook: passage of time, agenda, schedule, self-identity

Deep water: trouble

Demons: primitive instincts, repressed sexual urges

Descending: quest for self-knowledge, self-discovery, the unconscious

Devils: tempters, protagonists, seducers, negativity, hopelessness, falling out of favor; negative animus (the male element in female unconscious)

Diagnosis: ongoing analysis in dream

Digging: self-discovery

Dinner: emotional nourishment or protection, satisfaction of needs

Dog: Dionysian animal spirit, instincts, making friends with yourself, foreboding one's death

Dolls: babies

Door: entrance to illumination, imagination, opening up or closing off, forbidden

Doorknob: phallic symbol

Driving wheel: wheel of life, symbol of control, responsibility

Drowning: suffocation by system, being engulfed or overwhelmed, loss of identity

Drum roll: performance

Dust: layers of memory, veil

Edge: edginess, borderline

Empty hole: the unconscious

Envelope: deliverance, enveloped, consumed, sealed off

Excrement: death, decay, defilement, money

Explosions: sexual activity, ejaculation, orgasm, sexual climax

Extended objects: phallus, full growth potential

Falling: surrender to an erotic temptation, loss of control

Fertile ground: womb

Film: distortion, veiled layer, projection of fantasy, raises identity issues

Fire: frenzied or ceaseless activity, intellect, sexual energy, desire, passion

Firearms: phallic symbols

Floating: on top of situation, above surface, superficial, without depth

Flying: freedom, renunciation, independence, detachment, objectivity, defiance of rules, exoneration, elevation and ascendancy, establishing individuality

Flying a plane: control, making all attainable

Fly wearing a sombrero: Spanish Fly, manipulate and control via drugs

Food: emotional nourishment

Foreground: present life

Foreign city: womb

Forgetting: repression, frustration, fear of loss of efficiency or power of selection

Frog: evil spirit, historically linked to superstitions, something bewitched that was transformed for the worse

Front: the future

Front seat: womb

Frozen: stubbornness, resistance, rigidity, reluctance, inhibitions, fears

Garage: cemetery, graveyard, the underworld, the unconscious

Garden: cultivation of creative side, unrepressed nature, passion, spirit, origins

Glass: perception, clarity, transparency

Glass hall: perception of viewing or being viewed or watched over

God: the father, creator, eternal being

Going outside: independence, beyond confines

Grass blades: weaponry

Green: novice, unripe, unseasoned, virginal, birth and fruition

Green pasture: affirmative view

Guns: phallic symbols

Hair: strength, power; (if cut, castration, weakness)

Handbag: self-identity

Harsh light: harsh realization

Hives: anger, physical eruption

Holding back breath: not accepting a situation

Homes, Houses: the body, the personality, being, self, state of mind, the mother, security, refuge, (the more palatial the home the grander sense of self)

Ice: the opposite of an erection: something that becomes hard in the cold; without emotion; linked to death, in that death makes things stiff; (phonetic—eyes: being watched)

Incline: struggle, maturational process

Interiors: the mind, introspection

Invisibility: unborn, protection, attached to forgetting or being forgotten

Island: isolation, independence, inaccessibility, autonomy, the individual self

Jesus: father, paternal figure, the good

Journey: departure, death

Jungle: the unconscious

Key: unlocking of higher truth, understanding, opening up

King: father

Lake: reflection, giving surface view

Large audience: the eternal being, judgment, the desire to be heard

Leaning forward: letting go, trust

Leaves: something fallen; (phonetic—leaves: goes away, exits)

Left: the past

Light: consciousness, awareness, clarity, of spiritual matter

Lighthouse: empowerment, scope, self-illumination

Little dog: helplessness, the underdog

Losing a pocketbook: loss of identity, sense of violation

Losing a tooth: castration in men, being violated in women, a gap or void

Lynx: animal instincts, (phonetic—links: connective symbol)

Makeup: covering reality; (as in to make up: redemption, expression of sorrow)

Magazine: the self, storehouse of information

Male hostile forces: castration fear, castrating father figure; negative animus

Mask: disguise, persona

Medicine: corrective measures, guidance, problem solvers

Mermaid: anima figure (female element in male unconscious, goddess guide)

Mirror: self-reflection, looking for truth, imitation

Mist: blurred reality; (phonetic—missed: longing, yearning, nostalgia)

Moon: wholeness, luminous enlightenment, feminine presence, purity, ascendancy

Mother: one who births, rescues, creates, resurrects; mother's room; womb

Motorcycle: phallic symbol, sexual prowess, aggressive tendencies, drive

Mountains: obstacles, insurmountable problems, dominating presence, immortality

Mouse: prepubescent male child, phallic symbol

Multistoried structure: multifaceted personality

Music: passions, being transported, sexual rhythmic activity

Nakedness: truth, purity, birth, innocence, naïveté, exposure, origins

Name: recognition

Nature: essence, giver and taker, hostile or docile forces, unpredictability

Nature trail: road of self-discovery

Ocean: psyche, soul, unconscious depths, mother, death

Ostrich: repression

Ovation: approval

Parked car: deceased individual

Party: celebration of life, complicity

Passenger terminal: womb symbol

Pelican: scavenger, hunter

Pencils: phallus

Picture: the whole truth

Pimple: the wish to break out or leave, recognition of repressed anger

Playing: masturbation, motivation, free expression

Playing the game: living

Pocketbook: identity

Pool: the body's internal fluids, amniotic, above ground pool, pregnancy

Precipice: on the brink of disaster

Pregnancy: filling a void, creative process, body of work, (the death of a baby, the death of one's youth, fear of responsibility)

Profile: not the whole picture

Puppy: baby

Queen: mother

Radio: the mind, transmitted thoughts

Railway station: departure or fear of death, appraisal of destination in life

Rain: birth, nourishment, purification, growth, tears, emotional outpouring

Remedies: corrective measures

Repairs: emotional or physical imperfections

Restaurant: emotional nourishment, socialization

Road: quest for knowledge, freedom of expression, direction

Rooms: the body, the personality

Sand: restrictive side of reason, sterile, barren, abrasive

Scenes: facades, memories

Script: part one plays in life, meaning, ideology, philosophy

Sea: unconscious, immersion; (phonetic—see: understand)

See-through: truthfulness

Shoes: feminine genitalia, watching your step

Shrinking: sexual culmination

Silhouette: outline, only part of the picture

Skating: avoiding issues

Sky: without limit, open-mindedness, independence

Snake: temptation, transcendence over instinctual side, change, sloughing of skin

Sole: (phonetic—soul: psyche)

Space: void

Spear: phallus

Spheres: the world, seraphim

Spiderwebs: entrapment

Stadium: magic circle, mandala, wholeness, totality

Stage: set-up, platform for ideas, maturational phase of development, spiritual elevation

Stage manager: God, the father, parental figure

Stairwell: stasis, lack of extremism in either direction, moderation

Storm: stressful time

Striking: lashing out or not accepting

Summer: youth, blooming, burgeoning relationships

Sun: Christ, dawn, new beginning, the father; (phonetic—son: male child)

Surfaces: relating to sense of touch and feelings, superficial, to rise into view

Taxi: being transported, inside vehicle, a specific world

Telephones: communicators with the deceased

Tests: preparations, self-expectations

Text search: way out of conflict, looking for answers

Ticket: gaining admittance, approval, acceptance

Tiered seats: developmental stages of life

Tomb: womb substitute

Tower: body, aloofness, independence, spiritual or mental elevation

Tree: of life, creativity, fortitude, phallic symbol

Tree branches: offshoots, alluding to evolution

Twilight: neither here nor there, noncommittal, transition

Underneath: the unconscious

Valley: unconsciousness, mother, nurturing wholeness, depression, a low point in life

Video games: at the controls of life, maneuvered or maneuvering

Warm water: tears, rebirth

Water: birth, rescue, redemption, renewal, absolution, the unconscious

Waves: being swallowed up, washed over, waving, welcoming or dismissive

Weather: driving, changeable force, physical or emotional condition; (phonetic—whether: indecisive)

Wheel: the sun, divinity; (phonetic—we'll: togetherness)

White: purity, religious devotion, cleansing, truth

White House: the presidency, leadership

Windows: the self, the soul, eyes of the soul, opportunities

Winter: death or dying, what is forgotten or covered over, old age, the deceased

Wires: wired-in, connected

Wise old man: guardian, God, spirit guide, animus

Witch: anima, negative feminine side of psyche; (phonetic—which: involving choice)

Note: Because certain dream symbols are emotionally loaded for certain individuals, dream symbols cannot be understood as universally accepted truths. Thus, the dream symbols listed here are those that have already been defined in relation to their respective meanings within the specific dream narrations in this text.

PART VI

**Dream a
Little
Dream
for Me...**

57

Dream a Little
Dream for Me...

The time has come for us to go to sleep, but in our sleep what dreams may come? To ensure that we dream a wondrous creation (as all of our dreams are, nightmares included, when they are fully analyzed) we should, whenever possible, follow these possible routes to dreaming.

1. Take a long relaxing bath filled with warm water.

2. Anoint the water with fragrant oils—preferably jasmine, orange blossom (bergamot), or stephanotis.

3. Let hands and arms go limp.

4. Everything should be silent except for the sounds of classical music—preferably an adagio—wafting in through the bathroom door.

5. Close eyes and think of absolutely nothing (no easy trick, this!). Clear your head of ideas—just sense what you physically feel and hear, for about five minutes.

6. Sense the warm water on your skin.

7. Sense immersion.

8. Now you may begin thinking again. Think of a dream you would like to have.

9. Après bath, sit in your bed and imagine a big blank screen. Imagine presenting your dream on that screen. Think of your current stressors or a problem that needs solving. Ask

yourself how you are feeling. Ask yourself if you are angry with anyone. Examine your conscience for any guilt. Think of a desirable someone, new or old. The idea is to get yourself thinking. Thinking heavy thoughts before bedtime is a sure way to produce a dream because the unconscious is a workaholic that is skilled in problem solving.

10. Talk to yourself and *ask yourself for a dream.*

11. Say, in a calm, clear voice—"I would like a dream, please."

12. Order one in the way you would order an entrée—remember that you are hungry to be nourished and dreams are *food for thought.*

13. Tip yourself in advance—a dollar under the pillow will do.

14. Set an alarm, preferably a snooze alarm that allows you to go back to sleep and dream some more. (Being awakened by a noise usually helps one to remember that one was in the middle of dreaming.)

15. If this doesn't produce a dream, try eating some pickles!

Please note that if at any time you should ever want to rid yourself of a dream, there is a fool-proof method. Change your position. For example: If you are lying on your back, turn onto your left or right side; if you are sleeping on your right or left side, switch to your back. For some physiological reason the brain remembers or encodes the dream in a positional form, which means that any movement away from your original position during dreaming will do the trick.

INFLUENCING YOUR DREAM

If the purpose of dreaming is to improve the quality of life of the dreamers, the predreamers must ask themselves what it is that they want to achieve. For example, thinking of symbols of wealth prior to bedtime may influence the narrative script of the dream. If one envisions oneself as a wealthy and successful businessperson one will be allowed the experiential effect of unconscious empowerment, which will carry over into consciousness and serve as inspiration. One may manifest behavioral and attitudinal changes, be more assertive, and act with a newfound air of confidence, which in turn may make superiors entrust one with greater responsibilities.

Design of Process

consciousness: desire for greater wealth =
unconscious dream: experiencing wealth and success =
dream interpretation: conscious assessment of dream experience =
unconscious reinforcement of conscious wish =
unconscious experience expands conscious motivation

Now, until the break of day
I bid you on your trip away
When visions fair yet yield revisions
And flights of fancy
Mock decisions

Dream on

APPENDIX

DREAM JOURNAL TO RECORD YOUR DREAMS			
Date	Dream Narrative	Emotional Reaction	Antecedent

Date	Dream Narrative	Emotional Reaction	Antecedent

Date	Dream Narrative	Emotional Reaction	Antecedent

Date	Dream Narrative	Emotional Reaction	Antecedent